The Gita
within *Walden*

The Gita
within *Walden*

Paul Friedrich

Published by
State University of New York Press, Albany

For information, contact State University of New York Press, Albany, NY
www.sunypress.edu

Production by Diane Ganeles
Marketing by Anne M. Valentine

Library of Congress Cataloging-in-Publication Data

Friedrich, Paul, 1927–
    The Gita within Walden / Paul Friedrich.
        p. cm.
    Includes bibliographical references and index.
    ISBN 978-0-7914-7617-8 (hardcover : alk. paper)
    ISBN 978-0-7914-7618-5 (pbk. : alk. paper)
    1. Bhagavadgita.   2. Thoreau, Henry David, 1817–1862.
Walden.   3. Philosophy in literature.   4. Spirituality in literature.
I. Title.

BL1138.67.F75 2009
294.5'924046—dc22   2008005524

10 9 8 7 6 5 4 3 2 1

To Joan

Contents

Acknowledgments

I am grateful to the following students, colleagues, and relatives for their comments on various stages of various parts of this book—whether in written or lecture form: Gurcharan Das, Theo Dunkelgrün, Jonathan Elsworth, James Fernandez, Joan Friedrich, Rick Furtak, Richard Heitman, Katie Kretler, Tim Lubin, Kim Marriott, Michael McTwigan, Dean Moyar, Bruce Novak, and Manu Shetty. My paper "The Ganges-Concord Confluence" was read at the 1999 annual meeting of the American Anthropological Association in a panel on East Asian rhetoric organized by Barney Bate. Several versions of "A Poetics for Activism," "The Imaginative Act," and other aspects of the Gita/*Walden* connection were read at the University of Chicago and University College, Dublin, Ireland, between 2000 and 2005. Courses on *Walden*, the Gita, or both combined, were given ten times between 1998 and 2004. I also am deeply grateful to Katie Gruber for her informed, expert typing, to Maureen Mahowald for her assiduous library research, and to Peter LeQuire for typing and research, both excellent. I stand indebted to the following three for their critical reviews of all or almost all of the manuscript: Thomas Bartscherer (theory), Charles Comey (theory, Thoreau), Whitney Cox (theory, Sanskrit). Finally, respectful acknowledgment to the efforts of previous scholars who have dealt with the Gita/ *Walden* connection in articles or chapters and in one case

(Jeswine) a thesis: Anderson (1968), Cavell (1981), Christy (1932), Jeswine (1971), Hodder (2001), McShane (1964), and Stein (1963); particular respect goes to the elegant, comprehensive, ambitious (and generally ignored) little book by Dhawan (1985). Warm thanks also to the Lichstern Fund of the Anthropology Department of the University of Chicago and to the ready helpfulness of Anne Ch'ien and Anne Gamboa of, respectively, the Department of Anthropology and the Committee on Social Thought.

First chronologically but by no means last conceptually: a sense of profound indebtedness to Dick Karskaden, with whom I argued passionately about *Walden* while cutting out hurricane timber sixty years ago in The Cameron Woods near Concord River; to my political theorist father Carl Friedrich, with whom I discussed dozens of Thoreau questions, often while circumambulating Walden Pond; and the late Daniel Ingalls of Harvard University, who in his renownedly disciplined Sanskrit course burned into my brain not only categories of grammar but that the Sanskrit classics are terribly important. Last but most: to my soulmate Domnica Radulescu and my friend and daughter Joan Friedrich. I am grateful for all these debts—and the chance to acknowledge them.

Introduction

Farthest India is nearer to me than Concord or Lexington.

— Henry David Thoreau, *Journal*, vol. 1

I remember the book [the *Gita*] as an hour before sunrise.

— Henry David Thoreau, *Journal*, vol. 1

My basic goals in comparing these two great books are three. The first and least arises from an exaggerated but still valid dictum: "anthropology is comparative, or nothing." Second, the sheer details, be it in Thoreau's maples or Krishna's tusks, have the power to stir up one's imagination when they are lined up or played against each other—and just how was the mind of Henry Thoreau fired by sparks from the divine Gita? But beyond metaphor and inherent or intrinsic fascination, is the more basic goal of demonstrating how both books work toward deeper meanings of, for example, nature, purity, courage, duty, God. Such a work, fairly obvious for the Gita, has been explored by the great Indian commentators, Mahatma Gandhi, R. C. Zaehner, Hans van Buitenen, and a host of others. Such a work, likewise, has been studied for *Walden* by Boudreau, Cavell, Hodder, and many others, and needs to be adumbrated and made more profound.

What is meant by "deeper" meanings and values here? To begin, both books teem with insights about the human condition that are imbricated with the language of the authors and their respective traditions. From another angle, both books engage fundamental issues—often metaphysical or theological—of time, immortality, the soul (or self), duty, the supernatural, and courage in the face of death. But they also articulate, pragmatically, steps, advice and generalizations about how to live in this potentially joyous but all too often troubled or tragic world, and how to interpret whatever one has lived through and experienced. Such sweeping or generic import partly accounts for their enduring, worldwide popularity. (As a yearlong teacher of both to talented adults, I have repeatedly witnessed these more or less scriptural or quasi-spiritual functions.)

The approaches of the present book are through historical, philosophical, and aesthetic analyses that fall into nine chapters. I start with the meaning of "God" for both poets, coupled with a historical retrospect on the maelstrom of their respective sources—Buddhism in the Gita, for example, and the *Iliad* for Thoreau. Then comes a summary discussion of the total of twenty-two underlying absolutes, such as purity and the rejection of opposites, that are shared by the authors. I illustrate all this in chapter 4 by turning to an analysis of four complex master metaphors for both works: ax/axis/axes, the upside-down tree, the bean field/Field, and eye/light. There follows a discussion of social and ethical absolutes with a close look at three of them, notably the tension between a literary elitism or a sense of an elect versus radical egalitarianism—be it with the ordinary folk of Concord or the mankind accessible to Krishna. There follows an abstract chapter on reality and being, and another, looping back to the first, on three ways to God. The first part of the last chapter depicts in briefest compass the extraordinary projections of *The Gita within* Walden in Thoreau's exemplary political activism and, then, the enormous ramifications of this and the Gita itself in American and East Indian political history—notably the incarnation or personification of the Gita within *Walden* in the figure of Mahatma Gandhi. The end of chapter 9 summarizes and integrates the major dimensions that occupy the core of the book.

The comparability of these masterpieces is challenged and actually enriched by the raw facts about them, to which the reader should be introduced at this time. We have, on the one hand, an ancient, syncretic, and apparently timeless religious philosophy, sometimes called "The New Testament of Hinduism," couched in eighteen books of orally transmitted poetry, with great compression of meaning. The Bhagavad Gita was a late (circa 200 BC) insertion into the world's longest epic, the Mahābhārata, the latter composed by bards in a culture of local kingdoms between about 400 BC and 400 AD—granted that these dates are matters of controversy.[1] The Gita opens with two armies facing each other. The leading protagonist, Arjuna, sees teachers and kin in the opposing ranks, is tormented by moral conflict and, dropping his bow, refuses to fight. The next seventeen books detail a dialogue with his charioteer, Krishna, an incarnation of Lord Vishnu, who expounds numerous reasons for entering the fray—and for having faith. The Gita ranks with the Vedas and The Laws of Manu,[2] as one of the sacred books of Hinduism.

Walden, on the other hand, is the most brilliant in a larger corpus that includes four political-ethical polemics,

1. One scholar or another dates the Gita anytime between 500 BC and AD 300; Upadhyaya (1971, 19) prefers 300 BC, citing Buddhist influence as decisive, but the authoritative van Buitenen and many others prefer 200 BC.

2. An encyclopedic work of 2,685 verses from the second or third century AD, covering a vast range of social and legal matters.

an eight-volume journal, and three other books in a generic
travelogue genre, notably *A Week on the Concord and Merrimac
Rivers*. These works by Thoreau are densely interconnected
with the writings of contemporaries such as Emerson, with
(Puritan) Christianity, with Classical paganism, and indeed
much of world literature. *Walden* is cast in a highly poetic
nineteenth-century prose by a notoriously erudite, stylistically
self-conscious and modern individualist in a just as notoriously or at least ostensibly individualistic modern culture
and nation-state. Like the Gita, Thoreau's book starts with
the author calling on his fellow citizens to have courage
in the face of despair and, over seventeen chapters, leads
the reader toward faith in general and resurrection in particular. Both books, then, despite differences, have much
in common. Both enjoy what van Buitenen, speaking of
the Gita, called a "supreme scholastic and supra-sectarian
relevance" (1981, 6).

The Gita was composed by one inspired seer and then
transmitted until the eighteenth century largely by word
of mouth. It is still being so transmitted by rhapsodes,
and parts or the whole are known by heart by millions of
Hindus to this day.[3] As to the minority position that it was
composed, not by an individual, but by a bardic subcaste
or group, its aesthetic integrity, the consistent majesty and
inspired quality of its meaning, and its differences from the
Mahābhārata in which it is ensconced (yet which it informs
ubiquitously), all point to the authorship of one monumental
religious poet with the technical and conceptual genius of
a Mozart or Homer.

Thoreau's work, on the other hand, while mainly in
the tradition of written literature, began principally as field
notes made in the outdoors or just after, which were written

---

3. Here and elsewhere I use the classicist distinction between the "bard"
as original oral composer and the "rhapsode" as reciter/performer
by memory.

up and organized as journal pages, then often given as lectures, and, finally, wrought into essays or chapters, which in turn were rewritten and reorganized. Lectures and dialogue with friends and members of audiences were the limited but critical substance of his orality. Many of his contemporaries saw Thoreau as a bard of deep wisdom who, like the Gita poet, attained truthfulness through meditation and ecstasy, and Thoreau saw himself this way.

For both authors the poet-seer is semi-sacred and produces work in a poetic form entangled in the poetry of sacred texts: the Vedas and, especially, the Upanishads, for the one; Homer and much of the Western and Eastern canons, for the other. Both poets eclectically cycle vast systems of ideas into rigorously poetic form: the strict syllabic meter and the four-line stanzas of the Gita; the well-ordered lyricism and sculpted paragraphs of *Walden*; the phonically dense poetic textures of both.

Thoreau was always classed as a poet by Emerson and other contemporaries, notably Amos Bronson Alcott and Margaret Fuller, and usually by himself; as a judicious recent Thoreau biographer puts it, "Emerson may have over praised the early work, but . . . who, in 1838, save Poe and Emerson himself, was writing better poetry in America?" (Richardson 1986, 42). *Walden* and Thoreau's essays and prose poetry or poetic prose were by a man who was also a naturalist, scientist, and environmentalist. What Aldous Huxley said of Thoreauvian author Loren Eiseley is also true of Thoreau himself: he was "a poet's scientist and a scientist's poet."[4]

---

4. See Anderson (1968) for a fine exposition of *Walden* as poetry, but note that *Walden* as poem and as sociopolitically relevant are not necessarily mutually exclusive. In the same vein, Thoreau as flamboyant punster and verbal funster does not weaken or contradict the function of *Walden*, for many readers, as a wisdom book.

Chapter One

"God"

The morning wind forever blows, the poem of creation is uninterrupted; but few are the ears that hear it. Olympus is but the outside of the earth everywhere.

—Henry David Thoreau, *Walden*

I make my dwelling in the heart of all: from me stem memory, wisdom, the dispelling of doubt.

—Bhagavad-Gita, 15.15[1]

The argument or, better, the persuasive thrust of both texts throughout their eighteen units is that the Maker, Creator-Destroyer, Final Cause, First Mover, omnipotent and omniscient God, by whatever name or circumlocution, is "really real," as Alfred North Whitehead put it, and should be striven toward. This thrust or telos of the two books, obscured by differences of society and culture, language and idiom, and historical context—and also by the agnostic bent of most Thoreau critics—is nonetheless ubiquitous and forceful.

---

1. Uncredited passages from the Gita are my own translations. For *Walden* I have used Rossi 1992 throughout; see also the references in this volume.

Both poets arise in a context of competing religions or schools of thought, many of which treat of issues widely held to be religious in the colloquial sense of grappling with or at least touching extensively on the supernatural, the soul, creation and destruction, infinity, death, and ultimate ethical and metaphysical questions. The Gita, on the one hand, harks back to the Vedas, particularly the (late Vedic) Upanishads, the logic and systematizing of the Sāṁkhya School and its critique of the limitations of (the study of) the Vedas (2.42, 46), and, finally, popular and early Indo-European and even non-Indo-European religious beliefs and rituals (Zimmer 1969, 379–400). The even more eclectic and syncretic Thoreau, on the other hand, includes, among other things, several Hinduisms, several Chinese poets and thinkers, Islamic mystics, the Old Testament (notably the prophetic books), Greek and Roman "paganism," Christianity in its Calvinist and, within that, Puritan, Unitarian, and Transcendentalist versions (notably drawing on the Matthew Gospel and the Pauline Epistles), *and* the religions of "simpler nations" (7); within all this stands an absolute respect for the person and the story of Jesus Christ, who is never criticized, mocked, or parodied but, on the contrary, repeatedly set up as an ultimate standard for courage and integrity—as in the sentences outside *Walden* where John Brown is compared to him (see chapter 9 in this volume). The 287 "uses" of the Bible (Long 1979), while partly a rhetorical device to make *Walden* more authoritative, also reflect deeply held personal beliefs. When Thoreau objects to "ministers who spoke of God as if they enjoyed a monopoly of the subject" (103), he means that there is a God and that he is claiming his share in interpretation. As many have noted, Thoreau's masterfully multivalent and poetic prose enables him to undercut and deconstruct the icons and clichés of Christianity while at the same time affirming many of its basic values through an invigorating reformulation. As West points out pithily, speaking of Thoreau's punning use of Matthew's "men labor under a mistake"[2] (3): "His quotation wrests words from their eschatological context, giving Christ's advice a worldly twist, yet it invokes Christ's authority" (West 2000, 436), and later : "In one breath Thoreau coolly distances himself from hellfire Christianity yet also suggests that its sanctions are ignored at their peril by the lukewarm and those committed to such interpretations of scriptural texts" (437). Or as Cavell puts it extravagantly, "He acknowledges his relation to the Christian vision by overturning it, 'revising' it. It is his way of continuing it" (1981, 111)—"extravagantly" because Thoreau hardly "overturns" Christianity. Thoreau uses the word "god" or "God" thirty-seven times in *Walden*, sometimes as part of a popular idiom, sometimes with strongly religious meaning: "my hat and shoes, are fit to worship God in" (15), "trees which the Most High God has created lofty and umbrageous" (53), "I cannot come nearer to God and Heaven" (130), "Man flows at once to God when the channel of purity is open" (147), "the hint which God gives them" (210), and so forth.[3]

The God of both poets is characterized by infinitudes (see also the section "The Infinitudes" in chapter 7). First

---

2. The basis of this pun, skipped by West, is the Latin verbs *labor, laborare,* "work," and *labor, labi,* "to slip, fall" (alluding to the Fall of Man).

3. The often baffling scholarly neglect of the role of Christianity in Thoreau—that he was a thoroughly anti-Christian iconoclast, "no Puritan," and so forth—owes much to the position of the authoritative Harding (1965) and earlier Thoreauvians. The neglect is instanced by Richardson's otherwise generally superb book on Thoreau's "life of the mind," which rarely if ever mentions Christ, Christianity, or St. Paul! I would say, on the contrary, that Thoreau's mind was to a significant degree the scene of a lifelong struggle with ideas in the Bible; as Leo Tolstoy said of himself, "God and I are two she-bears in the same cave." Notable exceptions to the neglect of Christianity include Boudreau, Bush, Cavell, and of course Long (1979) and the authors of the three doctoral theses on which he drew. James Duban (1987) made a valuable contribution to the issue of the Christian component in Thoreau's religious outlook by defining its "liberal Christian context" and the key role in Thoreau of relating *conscience,* "the divine spark of divinity in man," to the elevation of *consciousness.*

among these is the variety of incarnations that, though infinite, never exhaust God: "All states of being . . . proceed
from me but I am not in them, they are in me" (7.12,
Zaehner); "Higher than me there is nothing whatever: on
me this universe is strung like clustered pearls on a thread"
(7.7, Zaehner). God creates these infinite manifestations
tirelessly: "If I were not to do my work, these worlds would
fall in ruin" (3.24, Zaehner). *Walden* and other writings by
Thoreau, for their part, not infrequently suggest a totalizing
creative power, as in, "Nearest to all things is that power
which fashions their being. *Next* to us the grandest laws are
continually being executed. *Next* to us is not the workman
whom we have hired, with whom we love so well to talk,
but the workman whose work we are" (90).[4]

Yet the great creator and maker, typically benign, is
also the great destroyer and annihilator, and a cruel one at
that: Thoreau at one point cites the long, curved bill of the
heron, apt for getting in at the anus of the turtle. The Gita
poet sings of Krishna as birth, rebirth, and procreation but
also in song eleven as a devouring maw: "I am wreaker of
the world's destruction resolved to swallow up the worlds"
(11.32, Zaehner), "I am death that snatches all away, and
the origin of creatures yet to be" (10.32, Zaehner). Thoreau speaks of or alludes to the total destruction of death,
including the death of the planet (169), while also voicing
optimism, even enthusiasm and joy, about life and growth:
"Remember thy Creator in the days of thy youth!" (139)
he exclaims, citing Ecclesiastes. Or earlier: ". . . the same
thought is welling up to its surface that was then: it is the
same liquid joy and happiness to itself and its Maker, ay,
and it *may* be to me" (130). Both poets, then, are acutely
conscious of creation and eternity, which they balance
with an equally acute orientation to death, destruction,

---

4. The Thoreauvian ambiguity involves the workman as creator, but, also,
because the *w* is in minuscule, the workman is within ourselves.

and oblivion. This consciousness and its references is the second infinitude.

The Creator-Destroyer as thus conceptualized is suffused with mystery. All the elements of experience—from the most trivial to the eternal questions raised by dawn over Walden or the thousand suns of Krishna's brilliance—have yet beyond them a mysterious truth. It can be intuited in moments of revelation and blinding illumination, but it cannot be known in an ordinary or rational sense. The divine that inheres in every individual makes possible a highly emotional if partial intuition of the cosmic divine of which the individual is a small but infinitely significant part.

One such mystery of the two works: their divine power is both feminine and masculine—that is, androgynous. In the Gita this is revealed when Krishna describes himself as both the womb of Brahman and the fertilizing seed. Together they generate the world. Or again, "I am the father of this world, mother, ordainer, grandsire" (10.7–8 or 9.17). Seven ultimate values as listed are all grammatically feminine and labeled as such: fame, fortune, speech, memory, intelligence, resolve, patience (10.34). In one of Arjuna's pasts he chose a female role (in the fourth book of the Mahābhārata). The androgyny that underlies the Gita is masked by an idiom and an ideology that are male-dominated, patriarchal, and warrior-oriented.

The androgynous and feminine stratum in Thoreau is more complex and widely exfoliating, ranging from the mainly female gender of Walden Pond to the entirely female gender of Nature herself (referred to as "she" and "her"), and to the numerous elements of female symbolism throughout *Walden* and his other works: the female spirits that haunt the Walden woods, the mother cats, partridges, and other wildlife, the mortally wounded moose cow with her calf that—especially the mingling of blood and milk—so shocked him in the forests of Maine (Thoreau 1988, 156). A pertinent passage runs as follows: "Many of the phenomena

of Winter are suggestive of an inexpressible tenderness
and fragile delicacy. We are accustomed to hear this king
described as a rude and boisterous tyrant; but with the
gentleness of a lover he adorns the tresses of Summer"
(206). Elsewhere, as we note in chapter 4, Thoreau speaks
of an "old settler" and a "ruddy and lusty old dame," paired
mythological images of creation and memory with whom
he loves to commune on "long winter evenings" (93). In *A
Week*, moreover, we read, "A Hindoo sage said, 'As a dancer,
having exhibited herself to the spectator, desists from the
dance, so does Nature desist, having manifested herself to
soul—. And elsewhere: "Nothing, in my opinion, is more
gentle than Nature; once aware of having been seen, she
does not again expose herself to the gaze of soul" (*Journal*,
vol. 1, 382–83).[5] Aside from the gender issue, this passage
reflects an Emersonian view of nature as benign, from which
Thoreau distances himself sharply at other points in *Walden*
(90) and, even more so, in *Cape Cod*. The androgynous or
feminine element, in any case, precisely because of its partial
covertness and mysteriousness, binds the Gita and *Walden*
in a peculiarly essential way.

That brings us to the final infinitudes. Both poets
variously articulate or allude to a supernatural power that
is present constantly and infinitely potent. In the Gita this
is sung in many ways, ranging from the one primal man
to the material cosmos to the total creative power, magical
and uncanny, that bridges between them, to the Brahman
as the One, to Lord Krishna who includes all of the foregoing: he is the knower of the field in every field (13.2,
Zaehner). These manifold claims and forms, which are dealt
with seriatim, climax or at least become focused at many

---

5. As Hodder (2001) points out, this passage is a conflation of two in
the *Saṁkhya-Kārikā* (four, actually: XLII, LIX, LXI, and LXV; see Larson
1969, 273); the spectator is primal man, *purusha*, who is watching feminine matter, *prakṛti*, the dancer.

points in the idea of the total loss of self absorbed in the One of Krishna, as in this stanza:

> Know that through lucid knowledge
> one sees in all creatures
> a single, unchanging existence,
> undivided within its divisions. (18.20, Miller)

Or, in the rendering by Charles Wilkins that Thoreau read in 1845–1847: "That Gnan, or wisdom, by which one principle alone is seen prevalent in all nature, incorruptible and infinite in all things finite, is of the Satwa-Goon" ([1785] 1959, 127).

Walden and other works by Thoreau, on their side, frequently speak of or at least suggest a single totalizing and creative power. Most of the things he says about meditation, inspiration, ecstasy, and serenity imply the intense reality of the sort of power, or God, at issue here. "In prosperity I remember God, . . . in adversity I remember my own elevations, and only hope to see God again" (*Journal*, vol. 1, 368). "I am a restful kernel in the magazine of the universe" (*Journal*, 13 August 1838). Other references in *Walden* include "the laboratory of the Artist" (204), "The Maker of this earth" (205), "Even he has entered into the joy of his Lord" (210, alluding to Matthew 25.21, 23), and "The Builder of the universe" (220). There is a marked increase in Matthian references toward the end of *Walden* (Preuninger 2004).

The One of the Gita and Thoreau is, however, qualified in two fascinating ways. "The Lord is in the heart of all contingent beings," as we have seen earlier, "twirling them hither and thither by his uncanny power (*māyā*) like puppets on a machine (*yantra*)" (18.61).[6] Thoreau, in addition,

---

6. The reading of this as a puppet theater originated with the great Indian commentator Śaṃkara (Minor 1982, 490); a *yantra*, support or apparatus, from the root *yam-*.

adumbrates his omnipotent maker with the uncanny—the
loon's wiliness, his own interplay with a rainbow, and similar well-known instances. In another kind of qualification,
however, Thoreau can undercut his sometimes rhetorical or
formulaic divinity with delightfully unpredictable caveats,
as in the doubled citation of Confucius: " 'How vast and
profound is the influence of the subtile powers of Heaven
and Earth!' . . ." but then, "It is an ocean of subtile intelligences . . . they environ us on all sides" (90–91). Like many
Indic texts, Thoreau himself entertains a complex supernatural where a transcendent God is counterpointed by a
plurality of spirits, intelligences, demons, and the like.[7]

   The God of these poets is not only omnipresent and
omnipotent but both immanent and transcendent. Their
God is immanent, on the one hand, because within all things
and emerging through them in divine power. To repeat: "I
am the Self established in the heart of all contingent beings"
(10.20, Zaehner). The lengthy string of figurative expressions
cited in the seventh song of the Gita—"I am the flavor of
water"—all unambiguously imply God's immanence. God
is transcendent, on the other hand, because superordinate
to all in the realms of the spirit and of the material world.
Arjuna: "You are the primal God, the primal person. You
of the universe are the last prop and resting place, you are
the knower and what is known, the highest home, O you
whose forms are infinite, by you the whole universe was spun"
(11.38, Zaehner). As for the scholarly concerns in both West
and East (e.g., Sharma 1986) over the "fact" that immanence
and transcendence contradict each other, in terms of one
kind of strict logic, both poets would seem to imply that this
is (a weak) instance of the divinity's more general power to
unite the contraries, opposites, and antinomies that underlie

---

7. Thoreau's pluralism, avoidance of conventional closure, and advocacy of
a middle way owe something to Confucius and Mencius; for general studies of this neglected influence, see Cady (1961) and Hongbo (1993).

human delusion. Both poets would seem to imply, moreover, that a general position, if it is truthful, will include some contradiction (Bhattacharya 1965).[8] When it comes to the differences between deism, monism, monotheism, dualism, theism, atheism, pantheism, henotheism, and all the rest, neither poet seems preoccupied with theological or even logical consistency in the overall context of the scriptural book (Olivelle 1964, 527–28), as contrasted with a concern for maximizing the truthfulness that inheres in a line or a sentence, a stanza or a paragraph. It can, in any case, be argued with equal logic that immanence and transcendence do *not* contradict each other.

Let me integrate, reiterate, and embellish the aforementioned points by an overview that is admittedly extravagant in Thoreau's sense. The two scriptures advocate a God, be it Krishna or Nature, seen monotheistically in a variously pantheistic, pluralistic, or henotheistic context. This God is immanent in and also transcends both the microcosmic and macrocosmic universes of matter and spirit, universes that are interconnected and analogous to each other in infinite ways. Individual entities are sparks of the divine One, but even in their totality they do not constitute Krishna or Nature, any more than flying sparks constitute the fire from which they come: there is always the unmanifest beyond. Intimations of an all-encompassing God are found in the Gita's song eleven, in particular, but God is humanly immediate and concretized in the form of Arjuna's charioteer. God is likewise realized in Thoreau's all-encompassing Nature, but in a double, Transcendentalist sense: first, his Nature is the "non-I" of many Indic writings (and of Emerson), but, second, she is also the more familiar fauna, geography, human

---

8. While this sort of idea is often attributed to Godel (for formal systems), it was also enunciated by Ortega y Gasset and indeed others before either of them. Tolerance of blatant contradictions is also a hallmark of the Koran, and of both Testaments, of course.

character, and so forth. Nature is concretized in Walden
Pond. For both poets God is symbolized androgynously:
Walden Pond is at times masculine, even with a beard, but
is more often feminine, as when her beauty as a woman is
extolled. God, essentially mysterious, is both creative and
destructive, benign and cruel, albeit primarily the former
in both cases, and is present everywhere as the supreme
power, knower, and actor. God can be reached through the
yogas ("disciplines") of action and engagement, in the quest
for knowledge and insight, and, perhaps most powerfully,
through faith and love—all three liberate one from delusion and ignorance (see chapter 8, "Three Ways to God").
Both poets, after all their subtleties and complex persuasiveness, advocate an arational, highly emotional, at times
ecstatic love and adoration of God. For neither, in contrast,
is ethical perfection central. Some of the aforementioned
components had come to Thoreau from Homer and the
Bible, of course, but his overall meaning of a final cause or
mover was singularly modeled on the Gita—one reason he
so praised its "stupendous and cosmogonal philosophy."

Let me conclude with a tropological take. Krishna defines himself by a long string of equations, mainly synecdoches: "I am the self abiding in the heart of all creatures . . .
the song in sacred lore . . . the ocean of lakes . . . the procre-
ative god of love . . . the vowel *a* of the syllabary . . . death
the destroyer of all . . . the dice game of gamblers . . . the
silence of mysteries" (10.20–38, Miller). Although not listed
that explicitly or all at once, Nature is defined and essentialized in a similar way seriatim throughout *Walden*, be it
the autumnal tints of hardwoods, or the howl of a loon, or
the eyes and what's behind them of an owl or a partridge,
the grandeur of the Gita, or the inherent wildness of *Hamlet* or the *Iliad* (see "Walking"; in 2002, 166), or the flavor,
purity, and many colors of Walden Pond. Beyond these fe-
licitous examples, everything in the world has a visible and
knowable part or aspect, intense and most meaningful, that

symbolizes, emblematizes, and gives us intimations of the worlds without and within ourselves that are but a particle of God, or as put more precisely in the last stanza of the Gita's divine tenth song:

> I support this entire universe constantly
> with a single fraction of Myself. (10.42, Sargeant)

Or, following Wilkins: "I planted this whole universe with a single portion and stood still" ([1785] 1959, 89).

To conclude, "God" in the Gita and *Walden* never means one simple thing. The idea of God just adumbrated should be seen as one of many or at least several that are involved. To limit ourselves to *Walden*, another equally powerful idea involves the devoted search for the truth about oneself and the world around us: indeed, Truth as Thoreau's God has been cogently argued (Bush 1985). Also contributory were ideas in the Rig Veda (O'Flaherty 1981). A third idea is that propounded by Jesus Christ in the synoptic Gospels, especially the Gospel according to Saint Matthew, which Thoreau "uses" dozens of times (Long 1979). There are many other such ideas of God for a syncretic and polymath believer such as Thoreau, for whom "God" is best seen semiotically as a Wittgensteinian family of meanings expressed in hundreds of intensely meaningful (for Thoreau) words and sentences, all of which, despite their superficial disparity, allude to an awesome supernatural power of some sort.

Chapter Two

Historical Retrospect

Thoreau's interest in this [oriental] literature was relatively short-lived and left no discernible literary results.

—Robert Sattelmeyer, *Thoreau's Reading*

The Unique Individual Creates Scripture

There is a rare bridging in the Gita poet and Thoreau between the way they draw on all scripture or at least great books, on the one hand, and, on the other, their creation of new scripture—in other words, between their signally original uniqueness and their rootedness in many antecedent sources. Let us review this interplay between the unique individual and his literary content as a way of understanding the creation of scripture; this will also integrate and anticipate many of the historical allusions scattered throughout pages that follow.

Both poets deeply revere sacred texts or texts seen as sacred, but the scope and function of the reverence differs a great deal. The Gita poet, to begin, mentions the Vedas many times—as a source of ritual action (3.15), as the leaves of the tree of knowledge (15.1), and as one of the terminal sets of objects that define Krishna (10.2, where the Sama Veda, not the Rig Veda, is primary). He draws extensively

on the (late) Vedic Upanishads, rephrasing or paraphras-
ing scores of passages, as Zaehner has demonstrated.[1] (The
Gita also reticulates at many points with the Mahābhārata
within which it is enclosed; McShane 1964.) Throughout
the Gita we find input from the sacred texts of Buddhism
(Dasgupta 1965, chap. 14).

Beyond specific sacred texts alluded to or named, the
Gita poet sings of the authors of such texts, that is, of poet-
seers like himself, with high praise. Yet he also goes beyond
them and is intermittently skeptical: by conforming only to
them and other "ritual lore," one must reenter the cycle
of birth and death. He who has transcended the Vedas, on
the contrary, is like a well past which the redundant waters
rush (2.46) or, shifting figures, like one who with the ax
of self-knowledge severs at its roots the tree of knowledge
with its Veda leaves (15.3). The Gita proposes new thoughts
"not in line with those orthodox Vedic specialists who could
think only old thoughts" (van Buitenen 1998, 12). The
Vedas, then, represent but a particle of scripture, actual or
potential. Anyone who can create new scripture deserves
high praise, never with irony.

Thoreau similarly exalts the classics while also speaking
of them skeptically at times. On the one hand, he writes of
these texts, "beautiful almost as the morning itself" (70).
They are absolutes of sorts, which call for being read "as-
tronomically," as the polestars of one's own personal destiny
that the happy few can know enough to sail by. On the
other hand, he may speak skeptically of the great books, as

---

1. The four Vedas, the earliest of which dates from about 900 BC, are
the sacred books, "the most ancient and conventionally the most fundamental scriptures of Hinduism" (Brereton 1990, 115); the Rig Veda
includes hymns on many themes, notably here creation, death, fire, "lost
in the forest," and to many gods, of which the one to dawn is widely
felt to be the most beautiful. The concluding part of the Vedas, the
Upanishads, composed between 600 and 300 BC, consists of fourteen
units such as the aforementioned Katha, about two-thirds in prose, about
one-third in poetry.

when he alternates between reading a page from the *Iliad* and a page of yesterday's newspaper or calling the Bible merely "an old book" (3). He tells us to go beyond the great books through faith in a seed and other signs of Nature. "Better learn this strange character which nature speaks today—than the Sanscrit—books in the brooks" (*Journal*, in Rossi 1992, 302). As Thoreau put it, "Who's writing Vedas?" which implies that nobody was, but that he was attempting to do so. Both poets actually succeed in their fascinating challenge of revering while trying to surpass the greatest classics. Both texts are thus peculiarly self-reflexive.

Complex Origins

As a prospectus of what's to come, let us itemize without much comment the awesome panoply of Thoreau's sources. (Caveat: some readers may want to skip this dense section and return to it after reading chapter 5.) Now, to enumerate: (1) The Bible in his Calvinist and Puritan tradition, especially the book of Jeremiah and the Gospel according to Matthew; (2) Homer,[2] particularly the *Iliad*; (3) Greek and Latin authors generally, particularly the satirists, certain Stoics, Virgil, and Sophocles' *Antigone* and Aeschylus's *Prometheus*; (4) Cicero and other Classical rhetoricians and some of their English heirs; (5) Confucius and Mencius (*Walden* mentions the former fourteen times); (6) the whole sweep of English poetry, notably Chaucer's *Canterbury Tales*, much of Milton and Shakespeare, the Metaphysical poets, notably Donne and Marvell, and the Romantics, Wordsworth and Coleridge; (7) German thought, of Kant indirectly, but mainly Goethe (optics, theory of plants; the

---

2. The English translation of the *Iliad* that he took to Walden together with the Greek was that of Alexander Pope, "the greatest tyrant over native American taste" (West 2000, 24).

Italian Journey gave some of the orientation of *Walden*); (8) his friend and teacher Ralph Waldo Emerson, who rivaled Thoreau in the creative use of Indian sources.[3]

Thoreau's commitment to the classics, great books, and sacred texts in general was part of a Transcendentalist commitment to (literary) universals as distilled in world letters. His attitude is summed up in striking sections of the "Reading" chapter in *Walden*:

> The oldest Egyptian or Hindoo philosopher raised a corner of the veil from the statue of the divinity; and still the trembling robe remains raised, and I gaze upon as fresh a glory as he did, since it was I in him that was then so bold, and it is he in me that now reviews the vision. (67)

Or:

> To read well, that is, to read true books in a true spirit, is a noble exercise, and one that will task the reader more than any exercise which the customs of the day esteem. It requires a training such as the athletes underwent, the steady intention almost of the whole life to this object. Books must be read as deliberately and reservedly as they were written. (68)

Or:

> No wonder that Alexander carried the Iliad with him on his expeditions in a precious casket. A

---

3. In the case of every source, Thoreau renovated and recoined, giving pragmatic flesh to stoic abstractions, using biblical exhortations to pry into biblical values, and grounding Romanticism through natural historical realism.

written word is the choicest of relics. It is something at once more intimate with us and more
universal than any other work of art. It is the work
of art nearest to life itself. It may be translated
into every language, and not only be read but
actually breathed from all human lips;—not be
represented on canvas or in marble only, but be
carved out of the breath of life itself. The symbol
of an ancient man's thought becomes a modern
man's speech. (69)

There were interdigitations, both profound and shal-
low, with other giants of "the American Renaissance." He
and Hawthorne were good friends in Concord; he set out a
fine kitchen garden for Hawthorne and his wife when they
moved into the Old Manse by the Concord River. He read
Whitman and visited him briefly in New York City. Melville's
Typee was important to Thoreau about 1852, while working
on the last stages of *Walden* (Richardson 1986, 219–20), and
Thoreau, in turn, was the model for one of the protagonists
in Melville's "*The Confidence-Man*": there are deep symbolic
relations between *Walden* and *Moby-Dick*, that is, for example,
between the meanings of Walden Pond and the Pacific Ocean
(Paul 1953, 351–53; P. Miller 1967). He hadn't read Dickin-
son, obviously, but she was one of his readers and admirers.
Intricate indeed were Thoreau's connections with American
political discourse, ranging from the high-level ambiguities
of James Madison's Constitution (Fliegelman 1993) to the
lows of local and state newspapers and gossip (Allen 1936).
On a lighter side, while sojourning on Walden Pond, Thoreau often played the flute, as he reports (117). While this
may have been modeled on the "oaten flute" of his beloved
Greek and Latin texts, most scholars (e.g., West 2000, 442)
think that his imitation is of the flute legendarily played by
Lord Krishna (in his incarnation as an amorous cowherd
contrasted with his martial one in the Gita) (Alcott 1863).

History of the Gita Connection

How did this Concord orientalism happen in detail? Let us review the story, which perforce will overlap with information on later pages. Thoreau's excitement over Indian classics probably began during Harvard and deepened while reading the Laws of Manu (Emerson's copy of William Jones's translation) before and after his trip with his brother John on the Concord and Merrimack rivers (1839); the eventual *A Week* contains six pages of praise of the Laws. A typical sentence runs as follows: "It seems to have been uttered from some eastern summit, with a sober morning prescience in the dawn of time, and you cannot read a sentence without being elevated as upon the table-land of the Ghauts . . . Though the sentences open as we read them, unexpensively, and at first almost unmeaningly, as the petals of a flower, they sometimes startle us with that rare kind of wisdom which could only have been learned from the most trivial experience; but it comes to us as refined as the porcelain earth which subsides to the bottom of the ocean" ("Monday," par. 44). This reveals much about the primal aesthetics of the young Thoreau, "primal aesthetics" meaning a theory of the beautiful that derives in the main from synthesizing two things: a "heroic," close, and inspired reading of great books such as Homer or Milton with relatively little attention to criticism or other secondary literature, and, second, a relatively naïve and unmediated response to nature—dawn over a lake. Of course, Thoreau read some aesthetics, notably Ruskin and Emerson, and he read a lot *about* nature, notably natural history; his close natural scientific study of fauna, flora, and the like was an analogue to "heroic," philological reading, both calling for "ecstasies of exactness" (Cavell 1981, 44). But beneath these sources were the two kinds of direct apprehension and the intuitions that emerge from their synthesis—and a religious faith in the possibility of such direct apprehension and of such synthetic intuitions.

As for Emerson, he had already been reading the Laws of Manu since 1836. By the early 1840s and through that decade, Indian texts, outstandingly the Gita, were being read and discussed widely and with enthusiasm by the Concord and Boston Transcendentalists, led by Emerson, who notes happily in a letter of 1843, "The only other event is the arrival in Concord of the Bhagavad Gita, the renowned book of Buddhism, extracts from which I have often admired, but never before held the book in my hands" (Carpenter 1968, 107). By 1845 he had read and quoted in part from five other Indian classics, the Gita five times, the Vishnu Purana seven. Three of his major lyric poems obviously derive from the Gita: "Hamatreya"; "The Sphinx" (about which Thoreau wrote a nineteen-page essay); and above all, his most anthologized poem, "Brahma" (cf. Gita, 2.18–19, 11.34, 12.19). Much of Emerson's philosophy is strikingly consistent with the Gita and this is even true of his essay "Nature," written in 1836 before the former had reached his hands. The key terms that fill his journals in particular seem obvious adaptations, even at the level of grammatical constituents, from the Sanskrit he didn't know, notably *adyātma* or *parātma*, "over-soul," and the idea that "I and mine" are illusions. Both Emerson and Thoreau after him inferred these ideas from the suggestive translations. "No one Oriental volume that ever came to Concord was more influential than the Bhagavad Gita" (Christy 1932, 23).

All this Yankee Gitamania was absorbed by young Henry Thoreau, still fresh from Harvard and, yet more intensively, while living in the Emerson house as a gardener, handyman, and family friend from 1841 to 1843 (he lived there again for ten months in 1847). The Gita, combined with Emerson's "Nature," sank deepest into his consciousness. "I remember the book [the Gita] as an hour before sunrise" (*Journal*, vol. 1, 311–12).

It was the Charles Wilkins (1785) translation of the Gita that Thoreau (having, again, borrowed Emerson's copy) studied with such singular enthusiasm during the summer of

1846 while sojourning on Walden Pond (Richardson 1986, 175); during his second year there he reports that he was reading it and parts of Homer, Ovid, and Anacreon—we don't know which parts. He eventually read "the divine *Gita*" in three translations, two English and one French, and studied it not only during his two-year sojourn on the lake but off and on during the seven revisions of *Walden* that were generated over nine years (Shanley 1957; Sattelmeyer 1990); the second English translation was read after the publication of *Walden*. Late in life, that is, in his middle forties, he had become renowned for his intimacy with Sanskrit literature, above all the Gita.[4] The praises that he sang are conclusive. A famous encomium runs, "Beside the vast and cosmogonal philosophy of the Bhagvat-Geeta, even our Shakespeare seems sometimes youthfully green and practical merely" (*A Week*, "Monday," par. 35). *Walden*'s hyperboles include this praise: "How much more admirable the *Bhagvat-Geeta* than all the ruins of the East!" (39).

For his penultimate, climactic parable Thoreau took the name of the artist of Kouroo from the second word in the Gita, Kurufield, which denotes its place of action, a plain in northern India where, many scholars hold, the memorable battle actually took place about 800 BC. Other specifics of the parable locate it in India, although the parable itself was invented by Thoreau (with input from other oriental models). After his intense orientalism of the mid-1840s and then a slight decline, Thoreau went back to these treasures in the early 1850s, notably to the Sāṁkhya-Kārikā. A symbolic climax of this return was the visit in 1854

---

4. Thoreau was keenly aware of the Sanskrit language, and alludes to it poetically ("In every man's brain is the Sanscrit"; 1980, 153), but, despite his love of learning and knowing languages, there were at the time in Concord or the Harvard Library no learning grammars nor, of course, teachers.

of the English orientalist, Charles Cholmondely, who had come to Concord to see Emerson but ended up staying in the Thoreau home about two months. Cholmondely took long walks with him, corresponded for years thereafter, and eventually sent him a "princely gift" of forty-four books of Indian writings for which Thoreau, in anticipation, built a box of driftwood (Harding 1965, 346–50).

The Gita was but one of a large set of Indic and also Persian and Chinese classics that Thoreau made his own or at least surveyed during and after the two years at Walden Pond; he refers repeatedly in *Walden* and his journals to the Upanishads and the Vedas (Dhawan 1985). In the years shortly after his stay on the lake he also read or reread parts of the great epic the Mahābhārata; the second of the Vedas, or the Sama Veda; the Laws of Manu (some of which he copied out or abstracted for *The Dial*); the dramatic masterpiece, Shakuntalā, by India's great Sanskrit language poet, Kalidasa;[5] "The Transmigration of the Seven Brahmins" (which he translated from a French translation); the Hitopadesha, a collection of Hindu tales; and the Sāṁkhya-Kārikā, an exposition of a rational school marked by the enumeration and tabulation of abstract categories but, toward the end, as noted, depicting primal man (*purusha*) as spectator of the dance of feminine matter (*prakṛti*). One of the pages that Thoreau copied out from this Sāṁkhya-Kārikā says much about the copier: "By attainment to perfect knowledge, virtue and the rest become causeless; yet the soul remains invested awhile in the body, as the potter's wheel continues whirling from the effect of

---

5. The fact that Thoreau would single out and study the story of desperate loyalty between the two one-and-only lovers is congruent with his focus on the corresponding type of lyric poetry intermittently throughout his life, (re)reading, in part memorizing, in four languages, many of the greatest poets of absolute love (see chapter 3).

the impulse previously given to it" (*Journal*, vol. 3, 216–17).[6]
He also read some secondary Indology, notably Roy (1832),
James Elliot Cabot, and Garcin de Tassy.

Yet amid the orientalist panoply the Gita clearly stands
out. It matches Homer and Emerson as rock-bottom texts
in Thoreau's search for values beneath the illusions embedded in language and embodied in the greed, hypocrisy, and
authoritarianism that is rampant in politics and economics,
including American politics and economics. The Gita pro-
vided Thoreau, not just with the number of partitions (18),
but with many of the planks and pillars in the temple of
Walden, a number of which are dealt with in this volume.
Unlike his sometime swipes at the *Iliad* and Emerson,
Thoreau never qualified, ironized, or parodied the Gita. A
synecdoche for the great books of India, the Gita was not a
first among equals, but a first among non-equals, supplying
the basis for many of Thoreau's ideas and images, as I try
to show throughout, and also functioning as a link in what
Hodder felicitously calls his "overall imaginative assimilation"
(2001, 178, 204).

Perhaps the most positive assessment of the Gita in
Walden is by the critical giant of yesteryear, Henry Seidel
Canby. According to Canby's biography of Thoreau, the
Gita was "Thoreau's text book" (Canby 1939, xvii), and
"his doctrine was that of the *Bhagavad Gita*" (388). Among
the basic sources it was the Gita "most of all" (189), and
the Gita with Emerson's "Nature" "went deep into his consciousness" (199). Finally, referring to Thoreau's attacks on

---

6. The sixty-seventh stanza of the Sāṁkhya-Kārikā actually reads as follows: "Having arrived at the point at which virtue, etc., has no further
cause because of the attainment of direct knowledge, the endowed body
yet continues because of the force of past impressions, like a potter's
wheel" (Larson 1969, 275). The Sāṁkhya-Kārikā, controversially dated in
the first century AD, is mainly concerned with salvation from "three-fold
suffering" through "discriminative knowledge" of the manifest/unmanifest,
the material world, and the supreme person.

slavery, "If Thoreau's new conception of force to meet force was philosophic at all, it was the philosophy of the *Bhagavad Gita*" (392). Thoreau scholarship of recent decades ignores Canby and his conceptualizations or at least his way of putting things, which do sometimes seem at least outmoded, yet many of his intuitions are sound, as when it comes to the Gita, and as compared with today's books of subtle metacriticism where the Gita is not mentioned once (e.g., Milder 1995)—or worse, where critics such as Van Doren (1916, 95) or Sattelmeyer (1988, 67–68) categorically deny the influence on Thoreau of the Gita, an influence that is deep and "genotypical" (Friedrich 2004).

Finally, the confluence of the Gita and *Walden* is essentialized in Thoreau's own eloquent paragraph near the end of his book, after some words on how the pure water of Walden Pond was being exported to the world:

> Thus it appears that the sweltering inhabitants of Charleston and New Orleans, of Madras and Bombay and Calcutta, drink at my well. In the morning I bathe my intellect in the stupendous and cosmogonal philosophy of the Bhagvat Geeta, since whose composition years of the gods have elapsed, and in comparison with which our modern world and its literature seem puny and trivial; and I doubt if that philosophy is not to be referred to a previous state of existence, so remote is its sublimity from our conceptions. I lay down the book and go to my well for water, and lo! there I meet the servant of the Bramin, priest of Brahma and Vishnu and Indra, who still sits in his temple on the Ganges reading the Vedas, or dwells at the root of a tree with his crust and water jug. I meet his servant come to draw water for his master, and our buckets as it were grate together in the same well. The pure Walden water is mingled with the

sacred water of the Ganges. With favoring winds
it is wafted past the site of the fabulous islands of
Atlantis and the Hesperides, makes the periplus of
Hanno, and, floating by Ternate and Tidore and
the mouth of the Persian Gulf, melts in the tropic
gales of the Indian seas, and is landed in ports of
which Alexander only heard the names. (199)

Chapter Three

The Case for
Shared Absolutes

L et us now sum up the field of absolute values—the basic worldview—of these two poets; the ethical and social values, purity, and the nine metaphysical and instrumental ones will be expanded on further in this chapter.

Some, like courage, beneath their seeming simplicity, entail differences of meaning that are decisive: when Krishna says that an act of cowardice would bring shame, he does so in the context of Arjuna's caste status as a warrior, whereas Thoreau exalts bravery in terms of his Puritan, Indian-fighting forebears, or of abolitionist John Brown in "Bleeding Kansas."[1] Other absolutes, such as sameness, are complex and could be profusely subcategorized; their elucidation and illustration motivates much of the Gita and *Walden*. Yet other absolute values animate either the Gita or *Walden*—but not both: "meanness" is Thoreau-specific, as is his stress on skill or craft; on the other hand, the Gita's repeated warnings against hatred (*krodma*) are not shared by the author of *Walden*.

The absolutes in question are differently related to those of other worlds of thought and belief. Many, such as faith,

---

1. The Kansas territory during the bloody and atrocity-marked civil strife between pro- and antislavery partisans (1852–1854, approximately) came to be called "Bleeding Kansas."

are shared by Thoreau and the Gita poet and elsewhere. Others are found in other philosophies or religions but, again, not in *both* the Gita and *Walden*: "hope" is crucial in Thoreau and Christianity as against reincarnation in the Gita and Hinduism (granted that Thoreau flirts with it, may give it some credence, and, as noted, uses it at times for "tropes and expression"). Thoreau owed significantly to Kant's ideas of the transcendental categories through which one knows a leaf, a lake, or other non-trivial and trivial experiences. Finally, the absolutes—and I posit twenty-two—adequately define both Thoreau and the Gita poet, although the list itself is not absolute, that is, closed—but they do not so define (the absolute values of) any other major writer, religion, philosophy, or worldview that I am familiar with (with the possible exception of Leo Tolstoy).

Having given you some sense of "absolute," it remains to provide a definition, or at least a working one, of this problematic and archaic notion. "Absolute" in the present context refers to values, beliefs, creeds, and the like of one individual or a group that, consciously or unconsciously, explicitly or implicitly, are taken for granted, not questioned but, rather, assumed and acted on: the Gita poet and Thoreau never question, for example, physical courage or the simple way of life. Of course, human nature being human nature, no value can always be absolutely absolute. But that absolutes are a matter of degree and probability hardly makes them less meaningful. The meaningfulness is tested pragmatically by the way it guides or informs action—be it Arjuna returning to the battle lines or Thoreau protesting the return in manacles of fugitive slaves.

Occupying a special status are three absolutes that are instrumental in the sense of being a means to an end. These are disciplined action that is indifferent to profit and fruits, then the knowledge (*jñana*) and also insight (*prajñana*) that is obtained through action, meditation, or inspiration. Knowledge is consistently and sharply contrasted with the sin of ignorance, be it of the lower castes or the "strand of dark inertia" (*tamas*) in the Gita or in Thoreau's fellow Concordians who don't learn from or even know about the Gita and other great books. The third instrumental value, that of faith and *bhakti*, is not only the optimum way to God, but involves the idea of love in many senses, some of which are indeed suggested by subsequent differences between *bhakti* cults and *bhakti* poets. I return to these three values in chapter 8. To repeat, the protagonists in both texts, Arjuna and Thoreau, move from situations of despondency, despair, or desperation in the midst of battle, literal, literary, or metaphorical—the field of Kuru or the mortgaged farm fields of Concord—to a denial of this and an affirmation of the opposite pole of peace and harmony through identification with Krishna or Nature. To move from one situation to its denial to the affirmation of its diametrical opposite in terms of absolute values is perhaps the most basic tension in both texts.

Thoreau's absolutes drew on Biblical, Classical Greek, and Kantian ideas, but occupy a complex and diffuse field of often multivocal nodes that are often akin to Buddhism— note Krishna's web—or Confucius, a Thoreau favorite, or, closer to his Gallic origins, the wisdom of Montaigne.[2]

Let us come near to rounding out the foregoing summary of absolutes by listening to Thoreau on a theme that is not typically associated with him: love. Not only does he

---

2. Despite many affinities with Buddhism, the Gita only names compassion once, Thoreau only three times in *Walden*, but then in special contexts: "I cannot but feel compassion when I hear some trig, compact-looking man" (45); "For a moment compassion restrained the latter's arm; but that was a short-lived mood" (185); "Compassion is a very untenable ground. It must be expeditious. Its pleadings will not bear to be stereotyped" (212). Thoreau got Kantian ideas mainly through conversations with fellow transcendentalists; some of them were steeped in things German, notably Orestes Brownson and Margaret Fuller. (F. H. Hedge of the Hedge Club taught German philosophy at Harvard.)

proclaim, "There is no remedy for love but to love more" (*Journal*, 25 July 1839), but, at the end of "Paradise (To Be) Regained" (2002, 60), he takes off with: "Love is the wind, the tide, the waves, the sunshine. Its power is incalculable; it is many horse-power. It never ceases, it never slacks; it can move the globe without a resting place; it can warm without fire; it can feed without meat; it can clothe without garments; it can shelter without roof; it can make a paradise within which will dispense with a paradise without."

While all this about love might strike many as yet another Thoreauvian *extra vaganza* (two words; see *Walden*, 216) or be condescendingly dismissed as irrelevant to the Gita connection, it is backed, grounded, and made relevant by three interacting biographical facts: (1) his early-on, absolute, frustrated, and lifelong love for Ellen Sewell (e.g., Harding 1965, 94–104; Richardson 1986, 57–62); (2) his repeated references to (bathing at) dawn and to being a worshipper of Aurora, with whom he actually brackets *Walden* in its initial and final sentences (as a well-trained classicist he knew that Dawn/Aurora/Eos was an incarnation of or at least strongly associated with Venus/Aphrodite, the goddess of love); and (3) the way he returned again and again, and probably half-memorized, great poems of absolute love in five languages, notably by Anacreon and certain other Greeks, John Donne and certain others of his time, Goethe, Tibullus and Catullus, and similar Latin masters, and Dante. The expression by these poets of absolute love for one woman was part of the deep template of Thoreau's mind, and the picture of him as dull to such feelings is as false as the stereotype of the isolated, misanthropic hermit spending his life in a hut. Absolute love for another human being is close to, is an analogue of, the absolute love for a god, or God, as amply exemplified by some of the Spanish mystics and the Song of Solomon—and, for that matter, the later, erotic versions of the Gita.

Which brings me to two points of criticism. First, in the process of redemption that informs both texts, the role or even the existence of absolutes has been bypassed or obscured for two reasons. First, when put simply and bluntly, they tend to sound like the naïve fundamentalism that they are not. In the second place, the texts in which the absolutes are ensconced or embedded are themselves hallmarked by consummate subtlety, learning, sophistication, and ambiguity. Most Western critics and commentators, responding to these qualities of the medium, have understandably become increasingly concerned with paradox and oxymoron, arcane allusion, and historical and other issues seen metacritically. They have in general ignored the fact that millions of readers in all continents except the Antarctic keep going back to the deeper messages of these texts. Why? Because, like other wisdom books, they refurbish and recoin absolutes felt as absolutes. The titans of Indian commentary, such as Rāmānuja (Sharma 1986), are more concerned with theological controversies and not with absolutes as presented here. Some recent commentators such as Gandhi and Prabhupada have, on the contrary, been concerned with absolutes in a way that overlaps with my own; see chapter 9.

Having made a case for the absolutes and their sharing, I will end with two qualifications and a suggestion.

Despite the similarities between the Gita poet's and Thoreau's meanings of the twenty-two absolute values, the poets do differ from each other in at least two fundamental ways. The first has already been mentioned here: the radically different contexts that separate second-century BC priestly and warrior castes (*varna*) and even earlier (800 BC) Indic texts such as the Upanishads from a nineteenth-century Yankee intellectual culture of Concord, Massachusetts, with its particular synthesis of world literature and philosophy.

The second apparent difference between the sets of absolute values in the two authors resides in their internal structure. Thoreau, on the one hand, exemplifies a passionate, apparently contradictory, unidimensionally scaled or parallel listing of values that might be called Abrahamic, Jeremian, Matthew-derived, or Pauline, or various combinations of these (Long 1979; Cavell 1981, 25 passim). The Gita, on the other hand, exemplifies a multidimensional mode set by orthogonally related variables where, for example, "purity" is not an axiom governing all Hindus but, as McKim Marriott puts it in his brilliant analysis (2003), a derivative, three-dimensional substantial variable that is especially suited to priests but not warriors or farmers.

In terms of this latter hypothesis, we are left with the fascinating possibility that Thoreau was at some level responding to the Gita's geometry. At Harvard, mathematics was one of his favorite subjects (taught by Benjamin Peirce, father of Charles S. Peirce), he was a superb, notoriously accurate surveyor, and mathematically based metaphors are scattered through his writings; for many readers the high point of *Walden* is "The Pond in Winter," with its detailed geometry and measurements; the maximized science of measuring finitude is synthesized with the poetic expression of infinity (Johnson 1991, 144–52). Beneath the wild, seemingly contradictory and sometimes roiling rhetoric of *Walden*'s surface, in other words, may stand a hidden, orthogonal structure of absolute values—to date totally unresearched or even noticed. This underlying orthogonal structure would account in part for Thoreau's enthusiasm about the Gita's "stupendous and cosmogonal philosophy." So mathematics may underlie rhetoric and worldview at the bottom.

Chapter Four

Life Symbols
That Essentialize

Any object, word, act, or thought symbolizes, may stand for something other than itself; we live in a totally symbolic world. Yet among the many possibilities, a peculiar force inheres in objects, words, acts, and thoughts that are as concrete as an owl's eye but, for some readers and auditors, also stand for values that are maximally abstract, be it the wisdom of Athena or the primordial realms of "a civilization going on among brutes as well as men"[1] (*Walden*, 182) behind that owl's eye. Such totalizing symbols congeal or essentialize or abstract the gist of connections that may be historical or particular to two or more cultural realms, or that span such realms at the universal level of the psychic unity of humankind. Such totalizing symbols bridge and synthesize the realities of worlds that are usually separate; they can involve very different kinds of knowledge: the eye of an owl, the eye of the water that is Walden Pond, the eye of God, the divine eye of Lord Krishna, the eye or the "I" of Henry David Thoreau. These and other symbols are also many-storied: a pitcher of water is Walden Pond, is Christ, is Christian love, is Buddhist compassion. Far from

---

1. Loren Eiseley (1978) enlarges on this "civilization of nature" in his remarkable essay.

there being no metaphors of metaphors, as Wallace Stevens averred, all symbols are implicitly metaphors of metaphors; indeed, one macrometaphor may comprehend many metaphors, as is illustrated by Stevens's own poem "Someone Puts a Pineapple Together" (Hintze 2002, 26, 41). Many of the metaphors in the macrometaphorical Gita and *Walden* essentialize in the sense just defined.

The foregoing is the epistemological and tropological context for the four master symbols dealt with in this chapter.

Ax/Axis/Axes

Cut down this tree
that has such deep roots
with the sharp ax
of detachment. (BG, 15.3, Miller)

This sharp ax of detachment ("disinterest" in Wilkins) that severs the deep roots of the *aśvattha* tree of knowledge functions as a central metaphor elsewhere in the Gita. The fourth song, devoted entirely to knowledge, approaches its climax with two metaphors in contiguous stanzas: "Even if you were the most evil of evildoers, you shall cross over all evil on the boat (or raft) of knowledge" (4.36),[2] followed closely by, "As kindled fire reduces wood to ashes, Arjuna, so the fire of knowledge can make all action ash" (4.37). These powerful images are deepened in meaning by the very last stanza (4.42): "Therefore, having slashed away the doubt that abides in the heart and arises from ignorance with the cutting edge (or sword) of knowledge, perform *yoga*! Stand up and fight!" What is usually glossed as "sword of knowl-

---

2. Uncredited translations of passages from the Gita are my own; see my note at the beginning of the references section.

edge" has also been rendered as "weapon of knowledge" (Prabhupada 1972, 85), and the Sanskrit *asi*, incidentally, may be cognate with our English *ax*, Latin *ascia*, and so forth; it is legitimate to assume a generic ax or cutting instrument similar to the early Indo-European semantic family of ax, adze, battle-ax, which shades off into the cognate scraper, and knife (Mallory and Adams 1997, 37–38). While admittedly not an Indo-Europeanist linguist, Thoreau, with his acute sense for puns, etymology, and the semiotics of early Europe, would have been conscious or at least subconsciously aware of some of these ax connections.

An ax and its uses introduce the central narrative of *Walden* as follows: "Near the end of March, 1845, I borrowed an axe and went down to the woods by Walden Pond, nearest to where I intended to build my house, and began to cut down some tall arrowy white pines, still in their youth, for timber" (27). As we hear this anecdote, the ax, and its meaning as a symbol of knowledge and sight/insight, begins to be revealed: "The owner of the axe, as he released his hold on it, said that it was the apple of his eye; but I returned it sharper than I received it" (27; note the punning on eye/I, etc.). Later the idea of the ax/edge/wedge of knowledge and sight/insight is developed more clearly:

> Let us settle ourselves, and work and wedge our feet downward through the mud and slush of opinion, and prejudice, and tradition, and delusion, and appearance, that alluvion which covers the globe, through Paris and London, through New York and Boston and Concord, through Church and State, through poetry and philosophy and religion, till we come to a hard bottom and rocks in place, which we can call *reality*, and say, This is, and no mistake; and then begin, having a *point d'appui*, below freshet and frost and fire, a place where you might found a wall or a state,

or set a lamp-post safely, or perhaps a gauge, not a Nilometer, but a Realometer, that future ages might know how deep a freshet of shams and appearances had gathered from time to time. If you stand right fronting and face to face[3] to a fact, you will see the sun glimmer on both its surfaces, as if it were a cimeter, and feel its sweet edge dividing you through the heart and marrow, and so you will happily conclude your mortal career. (66)

"Cimeter" in this passage is Thoreau's neologism for "scimitar," a curved sword (from French *cimeterre*, ultimately Persian *šimšīr*). Here, as has long been noted, it involves a paronomastic play on "see-meter," consonant with the Realometer, a device Thoreau has substituted for the ancient Nilometer (for plumbing the Nile). In the next paragraph we read that "the intellect is a cleaver; it discerns and rifts its way into the secret of things" (67).

The ax returns with the central visitor in "Visitors," a French-Canadian woodchopper who chops with deliberate artistry, beveling stumps to the level of the ground, for example. This woodchopper is associated linguistically with one of the key animal symbols in *Walden*, the woodchuck, named twenty times in *Walden*, including five times in "The Bean-Field." This tree-cutting or -chucking rodent,[4] which Thoreau and his woodchopping visitor were wont to eat on occasion, competes with Thoreau in consuming the beans

---

3. This and other striking occurrences of the "face to face" idiom *may* reflect 1 Corinthians 13.12: "for now we see in a mirror darkly; but then, face to face."

4. While the word "woodchuck" probably comes from a Native American word (e.g., Cree *wuchack*), it has long been folk etymologized with the meaning of woodchopper, as in the traditional tongue twister "How much wood would a woodchuck chuck . . . ?" Thoreau's philosophizing about his wood-chopper friend, Alex Therien, inspired Emerson's unpublished essaym, "Therionism" (Richardson 1995, 471).

of his field, and the beans themselves become analogues of the faith and trust that Thoreau would like to cultivate (see "Field/Bean-Field" further on). Chopping the weeds in bean-fields and chopping trees, both done deliberately, are related analogically to the deliberateness and piety of the artist Kouroo near the end of *Walden*.

In the third place, the idea and word for ax are connected poetically and onomastically if not etymologically with the geometry of axis and axes that keeps surfacing in *Walden*'s many mathematical figures and that is the focus of the in some ways central chapter, "The Pond in Winter," with all its meticulous measurements and their psychological and ethical implications: where axes of length and breadth intersect will be the deepest point in Walden Pond—and in a man's character (193–95). Axes, cutting, intersection, and related ideas in the half dozen senses adumbrated previously thus constitute part of the vast allegorical network that is *Walden* on one of its most meaningful levels, allegories and parables that invite the reader to a simultaneous reading of components that would have been kept apart by the linearity of the narrative (Nodland 2003).

Fourth and most profoundly, Thoreau takes his ax to go in search of water, "if that be not a dream," and, having opened a window in the ice with that ax, sees "the quiet parlor of the fishes" and "a perennial waveless serenity . . . Heaven is under our feet as well as over our heads" (188). This reversed axis (heaven as down instead of up), like the upside-down *aśvattha* tree and Walden Pond itself and the ax in question, can lead to intimations of the unmanifest beyond.

Decisive in terms of Thoreau's ax symbolism was his parable of the lost ax. One winter's day after he's tossed it down, "as if some evil genius had directed it, it slid four or five rods directly into one of the holes, where the water was twenty-five deep" (120). This ax, like many things named in *Walden*, is phallic: like the serpentine logs deep in the water of the upside-down tree parable, it "is standing on its head, with its helve erect and gently swaying to and fro with the pulse of the pond." Thoreau retrieves it with an ingenious slip-noose attached to a birch—presumably a birch sapling.

The aberrant ax, ignored by critics and commentators (except Williams), is, like the cimeter, a mythological ax of knowledge and maybe more because, at least subconsciously, it was inspired by or alludes to an equally curious incident in the Old Testament. In 2 Kings, the ax of one of Elisha's men falls into the water: ". . . when they came to Jordan, they cut down wood. But as one was felling a beam, the ax head fell into the water: and he cried, and said, Alas, master! for it was borrowed. And the man of God (Elisha) said, Where fell it? And he showed him the place. And he cut down a stick, and cast it in thither; and the iron did swim. Therefore he said, Take it up to thee. And he put out his hand, and took it" (6.4–7). Whatever the creative relation between the two authors, the magic of Elisha is, I feel, retained as a nuance in Thoreau, albeit masked by the forms of "Yankee ingenuity," which, at a level of moral lesson, replace or at least confront the prophet's magic of Elisha. In both *Walden* and the Bible, be it noted, the ax is borrowed, and the anxiety about its accidental loss is connected with the value for both authors of faith and trust. We have a confluence, then, between the Bible and the Gita in honing Thoreau's ax symbolism.

The Upside-Down Tree

Perhaps the most curious and diagnostic connection between the two poets occurs in *Walden* near the end of the ninth chapter, "The Ponds," with its local yarn concerning a yellow pine that once stood submerged in the middle of nearby White Pond, its severed end barely projecting above the surface. The pine was thought by some to be "one of the primitive forest that formerly stood there" (133), but Thoreau gets a different account from the man who claimed to have been responsible for removing it:

> In the spring of '49 I talked with the man who lives nearest the pond in Sudbury, who told me that it was he who got out this tree ten or fifteen years before . . . It was in the winter, and he had been getting out ice in the forenoon, and had resolved that in the afternoon, with the aid of his neighbors, he would take out the old yellow pine. He sawed a channel in the ice toward the shore, and hauled it over and along and out on to the ice with oxen; but, before he had gone far in his work, he was surprised to find that it was wrong end upward, with the stumps of the branches pointing down, and the small end firmly fastened in the sandy bottom . . . There were marks of an axe and of woodpeckers on the but[t] . . . His father, eighty years old, could not remember when it was not there. Several pretty large logs may still be seen lying on the bottom, where, owing to the undulation of the surface, they look like huge water snakes in motion. (133–34)

What is the source of this upside-down yellow pine and what does it mean?

At one level this is an intriguing bit of local history that, like a piece of amber, completes the jeweled chain of lakes, "great crystals on the surface of the earth" (134). At a second level, what Thoreau calls a yellow pine or a pitch pine (it was more probably a white pine) is a quaint local variant that reminds some readers and surely reminded Thoreau of the Tree of Knowledge of Good and Evil in

Genesis and *Paradise Lost,* or the World Tree in many my-thologies, Indic and otherwise, or the Bodhi Tree under which Buddha attained enlightenment, or perhaps the Old Norse Tree of Knowledge on which Odin hung (Thoreau was familiar with these latter myths through his study of ancient Scandinavian literature at Harvard and later).[5]

At a third level, of prima facie mystification, we cannot know and are not meant to, as with one of Thoreau's most celebrated paragraphs (see, e.g., Johnson 1987):

> I long ago lost a hound, a bay horse, and a turtle-dove, and am still on their trail. Many are the travellers I have spoken concerning them, describ-ing their tracks and what calls they answered to. I have met one or two who had heard the hound, and the tramp of the horse, and even seen the dove disappear behind a cloud, and they seemed as anxious to recover them as if they had lost them themselves. (11)

This would be a case of signifiers with signifieds that can-not be recaptured.

A fourth, realistic or natural, level comes from a sur-prising source, the founder of the Hare Krishna movement, regarded by devotees as one of the leading proponents of Krishna consciousness in the world. His work for the general public entitled *The Bhagavad-Gita as It Is* has this about the upside-down tree:

> Now, we have no ready experience in this world of a tree situated with its branches down and its roots upward, but there is such a thing. That tree

---

5. Elsewhere (in "Winter Visitors," 180), he calls the white pine a pumpkin pine; the Indic *aśvattha* becomes a fascinating case of *nomina confusa* in Concord.

can be found when we go to a reservoir of water. We see that the trees on the bank are reflected upon the water—branches down, roots up. In other words, the tree of this material world is only a reflection of the real tree. The real tree is the spiritual world. The reflection of the real tree is situated on desire, as the tree's reflection is situated on water. One who wants to get out of this material existence must know this tree thoroughly, through analytical study. Then he can cut off the relationship with it. (Prabhupada 1972, 228)

At a fifth, mythological level, the upside-down yellow pine is an arcane but recapturable allusion to the beginning of song fifteen of the Gita. In answer to Arjuna's question at the end of fourteen, Krishna says that the man who has surpassed material nature serves him alone, emblem of the immortal. He then continues in fifteen, as follows (in the words of the translation that Thoreau was using):

The incorruptible being is likened unto the tree Ashwatta, whose root is above and whose branches are below, and whose leaves are the Vedas. Its branches growing from the tree (are the material) qualities, whose shoots are the objects of the organs of sense, spread forth some high and some low. The roots which are spread abroad, below in the regions of mankind, are restrained by action. Its form is not to be found here, neither its beginning nor its end nor its likeness. When a man hath cut down the Ashwatta, whose root is so firmly fixed, with the strong ax of disinterest, from that tree that place is to be sought from which there is no return for those who find it. (Wilkins [1785] 1959, 111)

To complete the circle, or nearly so, Thoreau's upside-down tree most probably comes from Emerson's "The Poet": "... man is a heavenly tree, growing with his root, which is his head, upward." Yet Emerson precedes this with "Timaeus affirms," and goes on to cite George Chapman (the great translator of Homer): "So in our tree of man, whose nervic root springs from his top" (1940, 334), (actually, it isn't in Plato's *Timaeus* dialogue; Emerson may have been referring to the historian Timaeus [356–260 BC], whose work survives in fragments).

The upside-down tree has naturally provoked a long and fascinating tradition of criticism in India (versus the near absence of attention by American Thoreauvians). Some issues have been etymology, its relation to the world cycle and to Brahma, to a theistic cosmos and "ontic terror," all judiciously summed up by Arapura, who writes that it is "a symbol for the human cosmos (not so much the physical cosmos), the world of man, the endless round of birth, death and rebirth as well as old age, sorrow and bondage" (1975, 135). It stands not only for the "ontic terror" that moves all the cosmos but also the generic self-knowledge that liberates one from that dread. It could also stand for chaos.

We can never know just what this tree meant to Thoreau, but he must have been fascinated by the apparent contradictions from stanza to stanza between roots that grow up and then down and branches that are below, then spread, some high, some low, and the key idea that cutting through the tree—specifically its roots—with the ax of disinterest or nonattachment will give one access to eternity. His poetics of mythology hidden in parables here connects a humble thing like a tree sunken in White Pond (and like a night in jail for not paying taxes and other "most trivial experience[s]" [*A Week*, "Monday," par. 44]) with what he, as noted, speaking of the Gita, called "a stupendous and cosmogonal philosophy" (199). But whether the image of the upside-down tree came from the "divine Gita" from or without Emerson or from

Plato's *Timaeus* via Emerson or some combination of these sources, remains an open question.

The upside-down tree actually occurs early on in texts to which, in general, Thoreau often refers: the Rig Veda (1.24.7) and the likewise pre-Buddhist, late-Vedic Katha Upanishad (6.1):

> Its roots above, its branches below,
> this is the eternal banyan tree. (Olivelle 1998, 244)

The tree, finally, has cropped up in an archeologically attested ring of upside-down Druidic trunks that may well date back to the second millennium BC, in an Irish lake (Pryor 2000, 275–77). That these apparent cognates occur at opposite ends of the early Indo-European world practically guarantees the status of the symbol as Proto-Indo-European, which would have delighted Henry Thoreau in terms of his lively and well-known interest in the historical linguistics of his day.

The Field (*kshetra*)/"The Bean-Field"

The field-knower and the field of what can be known, both in two senses, are not only critical in themselves, but critically connect between the two poets and their texts, texts which, because the ideas in question are partly concealed, have confused major specialists. The Gita's thirteenth song, to begin, devoted entirely to such ideas, proclaims that the field comprises all the material world, including psychological values such as the eleven senses and ethical ones, often Buddhist ones such as nonviolence, and absence of individuality:

> The field contains the great elements,
> individuality, understanding,

unmanifest nature, the eleven senses,
and the five sense realms.

Longing, hatred, happiness, suffering,
bodily form, consciousness, resolve,
thus is this field with its changes
defined in summary.

Knowledge means humility,
sincerity, nonviolence, patience,
honesty, reverence for one's teacher,
purity, stability, self-restraint;

Dispassion toward sense objects,
and absence of individuality,
seeing the defects in birth, death,
old age, sickness, and suffering;

Detachment, uninvolvement
with sons, wife, and home,
constant equanimity
in fulfillment and frustration . . . (13: 5–9, Miller)

Wilkins's translation of the last three stanzas goes like this:
"Gnan or wisdom, is freedom from self-esteem, hypocrisy and
injury; patience, rectitude, respect for masters and teachers,
chastity, steadiness, self-constraint, disaffection for the objects
of the senses, freedom from pride, and constant attention
to birth, decay, sickness, pain and defects; exemption from
attachments and affection for children, wife, and home; a
constant evenness of temper upon the arrival of every event,
whether longed for or not" ([1785] 1959, 102).

Other parts of the field are philosophical or theological, involving, for example, absolute devotion to a supreme
spirit, or a material reality that goes beyond the darkness
that itself lies beyond the light that is visible to us:

Unwavering devotion to me
with singular discipline;
retreating to a place of solitude,
avoiding worldly affairs;

Persistence in knowing the self,
seeing what knowledge of reality means—
all this is called knowledge,
the opposite is ignorance. (13: 10–11, Miller)

This total field is known by the supreme knower, the supreme person or God who surveys and judges ourselves
and all of this material world. But then on a lower level
of this same exposition, the field-knower is also said to be
an actual person or worshipper who can perceive part of
the unified field and the boundary between the field and
the field-knower:

Arjuna, know that anything
inanimate or alive with motion
is born from the union
of the field and its knower.
. . . .
They reach the highest state
who with the eye of knowledge know
the boundary between the knower and its field,
and the freedom creatures have from nature.
(13: 26, 34, Miller)

Far from being "the most confused" song (Zaehner
1973, 332), thirteen gives us another poetic angle on one
of the main concerns in the Gita and *Walden*: knowledge.
The fact that the Gita gets to us through inspired wisdom
whereas *Walden* often riddles in parables should not ob-
scure the intensity and scope of their concern with striving
for knowledge, of virtue, psyche, and the material world

(including the material body)—nor the degree to which this concern is shared.

Thoreau's chapter, on a distinct but analogous track, first of all strings along dozens of bean-field realia in a marvelously associative way: perched above the sweating poet/hoer of beans, a brown thrasher sings like an amateur Paganini, and the bean-field itself is a metaphor for the Trojan War, with weeds toppling like Trojan warriors. Thoreau hoes a field of beans in the morning dew, with squirrels nearby and the sounds of Concord far away, and, in parody of Ben Franklin, casts up accounts meticulously down to the last half-penny. He will "finish his labor with every day, relinquishing all claim to the produce of his fields, and sacrificing in his mind not only his first but his last fruits also" (112). Beneath all this Thoreau himself is the exemplary, actual person who is striving for knowledge: "What shall I learn of beans?" (104) he asks, and then, "I was determined to know beans" (108). As the chapter exfoliates, these beans morph into complex metaphors for Thoreau's favorite virtues, all of them consonant with the Gita, including its Buddhistic ones, such as "sincerity, truth, simplicity, faith, innocence, and the like" (108), and later, "trust and magnanimity" (112). The beans of our Concord cultivator, then, are not needed in a practical sense (he cites Pythagoras's rule against eating them), but are grown "if only for the sake of tropes and expression" (109), for the sake of connecting the wild and the cultured, individual and cosmos. Consonant with this, Thoreau's one and a half acres of beans become in his reader's imagination a concrete symbol of the world, a world known by the higher maker who makes us all. This maker is only named later, but Thoreau gives us intimations in some of *Walden*'s most achieved sentences:

> The night-hawk circled overhead in the sunny afternoons—for I sometimes made a day of it—like

a mote in the eye, or in heaven's eye, falling from time to time with a swoop and a sound as if the heavens were rent, torn at last to very rags and tatters, and yet a seamless cope remained; small imps that fill the air and lay their eggs on the ground on bare sand or rocks on the tops of hills, where few have found them; graceful and slender like ripples caught up from the pond, as leaves are raised by the wind to float in the heavens; such kindredship is in Nature. The hawk is aerial brother of the wave which he sails over and surveys, those his perfect air-inflated wings answering to the elemental unfledged pinions of the sea. Or sometimes I watched a pair of hen-hawks circling high in the sky, alternately soaring and descending, approaching and leaving one another, as if they were the imbodiment of my own thoughts. (107)

The eye of Thoreau's sun "looks on our cultivated fields and on the prairies and forests without distinction" (112), just as the Gita's sun "illuminates the whole world" (13.33).[6]

Yet together with such ecstatic visions Thoreau, unlike the Gita poet, also weaves in a mood of conflict and question:

This further experience also I gained. I said to myself, I will not plant beans and corn with so much industry another summer, but such seeds, if the seed is not lost, as sincerity, truth, simplicity,

---

6. A co-source for this expression could be Matthew: ". . . for he maketh the sun to rise on the evil and on the good, and seweth rain on the just and the unjust" (5.45); Thoreau on the all-illuminating sun actually draws on four passages in the First Evangelist (Preuninger 2004). In general, Thoreau's "Bean-Field" chapter and other segments in *Walden* owe much to the parable of the sower (Matthew 13.1–30; Mark 4.3–20).

faith, innocence, and the like, and see if they
will not grow in this soil, even with less toil and
manurance, and sustain me, for surely it has not
been exhausted for these crops. Alas! I said this
to myself; but now another summer is gone, and
another, and another, and I am obliged to say to
you, Reader, that the seeds which I planted, if
indeed they *were* the seeds of those virtues, were
wormeaten or had lost their vitality, and so did
not come up. (110)

What was the meaning of all this, be it beans or virtues?

Thoreau's and the Gita poet's field-knowers both perceive and illuminate their respective fields with the eye of
knowledge. Both poets, in the course of the respective texts,
become more and more knowers, in many senses, of "the
field" in even more senses. Thoreau moves upward in his
chapter from concrete beans and the hoeing of them to
intimations of an infinite, transcendental spirit, whereas the
Gita poet holds his course on a philosophical level while
alluding to the way his abstract field is connected with
the actual, concrete battlefield of Kuru, named *Kurukshetra*,
the first word in the Celestial Song and, like Thoreau's
modest acres, an allegory for the field of life—or so it
has been understood by Mahatma Gandhi and many wise
listeners.

Eye and Light

Eye

A lake . . . is earth's eye; looking into which the
beholder measures the depth of his own nature.
(*Walden*, 125)

The eye, whether literal or figurative, and the complex concentricities that surround it, is another one of the deep symbols shared by the two poets. The role of the eye in the Gita is prefigured earlier in the Mahābhārata when the legendary bard, whose name is also Krishna, gives the narrator, Sanjaya, a divine eye so that he will be able to see what Arjuna eventually does see in the epiphany in book eleven. The power of the eye or, more generally, of the optic faculty, the faculty of vision, is prefigured by three other kinds of definition, all of them purely verbal in power: metaphor, synecdoche, and the best of a set ("I am . . . the [sacred] syllable OM" [9.17, Miller]). They are particularly inadequate for knowing Krishna. We return to them later (see "Essence and Tropology" in chapter 7).

When we get to song eleven, Arjuna asks, "I wish to see your form in all its majesty, Krishna, Supreme among Men. If you think I can see it, reveal to me your immutable self," to which Krishna responds, "But you cannot see me with your own eye; I will give you a divine eye to see the majesty of my discipline" (11.3–4, 8, Miller). And then Arjuna does see all: anatomy, weapons, society, the light of a thousand suns, armies disappearing into Krishna's maw, and so forth—far more than any human eye could compass. Arjuna wants to get close to or identify with Krishna through total worship (*bhakti*—see chapter 8), but the same divine eye that he has been given also enables him to see his own self and his own doom—and its inevitability. His divine eye from Krishna sees two ways: into himself and out into the universe.

In *Walden* also, sight outranks the other senses and, by figures that go beyond the Gita's, becomes a totalizing condensation symbol that pulls together, integrates, and hence condenses an open-ended or unbounded totality—in a bird, for example the owl, "with half-shut eyes, looking out from the land of dreams" (177), or better, the partridge:

"The remarkably adult yet innocent expression of their open and serene eyes is very memorable. All intelligence seems reflected in them. They suggest not merely the purity of infancy, but a wisdom clarified by experience. Such an eye was not born when the bird was, but is coeval with the sky it reflects" (152). These eyes are situated between the observing Thoreau and the civilization of nature.

More strikingly, the lake, its shoreline and shore path, its rim of surrounding stones and trees, even "the eye of heaven" above it, analogize the author's eyes and the author himself. "A lake is the landscape's most beautiful and expressive feature. It is earth's eye; looking into which the beholder measures the depth of his own nature. The fluviatile trees next the shore are the slender eyelashes which fringe it, and the wooded hills and cliffs around are its overhanging brows" (125). This intense circumposition of apt metaphors ripples out sideways to the greens and pure blues of the lake, the geometry of circles and their metaphysics. Similar extravagant figures, especially puns, involve seeing, the seer, sight and insight, vision and divided (*de-videre*) vision, all implying a double vision hovering between the material and the spiritual, the subjective and the objective, the inner and the outer, a "point of view" that is both the point where you stand and the point where what you see converges, a seeing, in other words, that is attuned to inner and outer form (Johnson 1991, 44). Walden Pond, "the earth's eye," is both a part and a mirror of God, that is, of Nature. *Walden* like the Gita is a visionary scripture.

Both poets play on the deep connections, etymological and otherwise, between seeing and knowing. In Sanskrit, including that of the Gita, the derivations from "see" (usually "find") (*vid-*) and "know" (*ved-*) are so interlaced that they feed into each other in the reader's mind (the cognates in English include "video" from Latin and the Germanic "wit" and "wisdom") (Mallory and Adams 1997, 337). Knowledge and insight are synthesized in the Gita's concept of "the eye of knowledge" or "the knowledge-eye" that, like unattached action or meditation, can lead one to supreme heights:

> They who through the knowledge-eye
> know what separates the knower from the field
> and the liberation of beings from material nature
> go to the highest and supreme. (13.34)

Thoreau in a similar way connects wisdom or knowledge with vision through his unique pun of the cimeter (see-meter) of reality, already discussed here.[7]

Light

> Out of my compassion (trembling), I, who dwell
>   deep within
> myself and in the hearts of my devotees, do
>   destroy all
> darkness born of ignorance with the bright lamp
>   of the
> knowledge of God. (BG, 10.11)[8]

That light and what is connected with it are a deep source for both poets is no simple matter. On the one hand, light is mainly mythological in the Gita. Thoreau, on the other hand, thinks of light mainly in terms of scientific descriptions and optics, and of how light mediates between the objective and the subjective, the material and the spiritual, the natural

---

7. In exploiting the deep flow between sight and knowledge, vision and wisdom, both poets with sound instinct are harking back to the early Indo-European root, *wid-*, which has both meanings and similar connotations.

8. This paradoxical line supposedly combines and reconciles Krishna's compassion for his devotees and his simultaneous and generic nonattachment (Minor 1982, 311 or 361; see also Gita 18.9, 26, 30, 33, 37).

and the sublime. Where and how do the two poetic visions, the mythological and the partly scientific, intersect?

In the Gita "light" (*bhās-*) and the allied "brilliance" (*tejas*) typify warriors with their "fiery courage and energy," and the priestly caste with its knowledge and lucidity—two basic components of the material world. Light in either case is emphatically and repeatedly counterposed to the ignorance and sloth or "dark inertia" (Miller 1986, 167) of artisans and merchants in the third strand. Gitaesque fire is consistently associated with the primary value of knowledge, as in the passage from the tenth chapter quoted earlier. At a higher level, light is the most essential property of Krishna, the light within fire, brighter than the sun and moon, a light, in fact, beyond the sun and the moon, the brightest possible light, brighter than any light that could be beheld or even imagined, as in 11.12:

> Of a thousand suns in the sky
> > If suddenly should burst forth
> The light, it would be like
> > Unto the light of the exalted one. (Edgerton)

Light, synergistic with ubiquity, infinitude, and primacy, helps define Krishna's awesome power, as in 11.47:

> By me showing grace to thee, Arjuna, this
> > Supreme force has been manifested by my
> > own mysterious power;
> (This form) made up of splendor, universal,
> > infinite, primal,
> > Of mine, which has never been seen before
> > by any other than thee. (Edgerton)

Light plays a key role in *Walden* (and other works by Thoreau), from the initial chanticleer crowing in the primal and mysterious light of dawn to the equally mysterious morning star of hope and courage in the book's last sentence. Light in one of its most beautiful manifestations, the rainbow, is often named in the journals and occurs in *Walden*'s "halo of light," which at one point surrounds Thoreau (as it did Benvenuto Cellini), making him "fain fancy myself one of the elect" (136); the rainbow is "God's face" and light was "the natural expression of Thoreau's transcendent God" (Schneider 1975, 70–71). As Thoreau put it, "Light is the shadow of God's brightness, who is the light of light" (*Journal*, vol. 4, 304).[9]

Narrowing or zooming in from these comprehensive views are Thoreau's fascinating observations on the originality of reflections, particularly multiple reflections that exaggerate, intensify, and reveal color, multiple reflections, that is, that enable one to see from many points of view and that result in "a permanent piece of realism" (quoted in Schneider 1975, 73)—for the seer with the eyes for these reflections. We see in the reflection that which we do not see in the substance. These and other of Thoreau's ideas are given additional purchase by the way reflections and echoes naturally provide metaphors for each other—as do crystallization and exfoliation. Reflections in these rich senses express the full nuance of God's glory in the natural world; recurring to our initial point on light's position between the material and the spiritual, "light itself is the phenomenon," as Schneider puts it. Light, especially blue lights and the light of rainbows, like the thousand suns of Krishna, symbolizes God. As *Walden* draws its curtain, "The light which puts out our eyes is darkness to us. Only that day dawns to which we are awake. There is more day

---

9. The biblical "light of light, very light of very light" is unquestionably the source for the "light of light" quote.

to dawn. The sun is but a morning star" (223).[10] Abstract religious and strictly scientific ideas of light are reconciled in Thoreau.

Let us conclude with two more observations that integrate the Gita and *Walden*. Light in both poets consistently intersects with the coordinate values of heat (*tapas*) and "vital heat." In the Gita both heat and light are associated with natural fire, ritual or sacrificial fire, the cosmos, and yogic practices of meditation and fasting that will liberate one from the biomental tyranny of pain and pleasure (Stein 1963, 46). The tropic group of vital heat and the corresponding inner light in *Walden* runs from clothes, housing, and food, to wood, local arson, and the Native American potlatch, to his great poem, "Smoke" (the jewel in his "House-Warming" chapter), to "perpetual morning," to the gradual shift in the central chapters from outer, seasonal heat to the inner heat of his cabin and the vital heat of his soul (Johnson 1991, 135–44). As Comey concludes, vital heat, above all fire, is "a sort of essentialization of creativity." Thoreau's excitement about seeing light in a most comprehensive sense culminates in a reformation of vision: "It is something to be able to paint a particular picture . . . but it is far more glorious to carve and paint the very atmosphere and medium through which we look, which morally we do" (61).

The aforementioned can be further integrated in terms of other dimensions of light shared by the two poets. For the Gita and Thoreau the sun is an ambiguous master symbol, be it Krishna's blinding brilliance or the soft light at dusk that swathes Walden Pond. For both poets light is a way of visualizing society or interpreting it and related ethical matters metaphorically: the illuminated virtue of the elect versus the sins of ignorance and illusion of the

---

10. There is a case for Revelation 2.28 and 22.16 being an additional source for this remarkable finale (Long 1979, 341). The finale is discussed elsewhere in the present volume.

tenebrous lower levels. Beyond this, light defines the seer, who, like Thoreau's owl, is awake and sees while others are plunged in darkness and who retreats into the land of an imaginative nod while others pursue mundane tasks in the light of day. Light and the light beyond light, finally, is the essence of the divine.

The four complex symbols outlined here are vivid enough inherently, but how do their meanings bear on the Gita/ *Walden* connection? What issues of method, of the comparative method in semiotics, do they stir up? Perhaps to be preferred as an ideal would be the method of triangulation, where at least three sets of phenomena are counterposed remorselessly in a much larger context, even that of a world sample. Yet here we have not a plurality of languages, cultures, or histories, but only two texts, each relatively capable of standing alone, and their respective poets (already compared here), one familiar in enormous biographical nuance, the other known no more than Homer, which means not at all. What have emerged so far in my disquisition are four symbols—images if you will—which happen to be metaphorical in the usual sense but are, as will be shown, balanced if not outweighed by other figures, notably synecdoche, moods (religious awe, devotion, and ecstasy), and the formal (e.g., syntactic and lexical) pyrotechnics of both authors (Friedrich 1991). The four symbols and the figures synergistic with them reflect and enliven the twenty-two ethical and metaphysical values of the two texts that lie so deep and are so constant as to merit being termed absolute (see chapter 3). The four master symbols are at one turn specific to cultural or even individual situations: Thoreau's concern with the science of optics, for example, or the Gita poet's assumption that caste is part of material nature. At another, equally significant level, all four images can be interpreted, after adjustments, as (necessarily) probabilistic universals that transcend individual and culture. No person on this planet would find meaningless a brilliant light, a slicing edge, a plant that was upside down, or the field of immediate experience of the sky, or of delusion or hypocrisy.

Chapter Five

Social and Ethical Absolutes

As will be argued in this chapter, the Gita and Thoreau share a critical level of social and ethical absolutes, in the sense of values that are straightforwardly affirmed and rarely questioned, mocked, or parodied; when they are, the underlying, positive take is not negated. About half of them pertain to acting in society, be it as a member of a Hindu warrior caste or as a citizen of Concord, Massachusetts. Let us review part of this field briefly by way of introduction.

The value of *chastity* enjoins a life free from the attractions and entanglements of desire, particularly sensuous lust (*kāma*). The value of *courage* tells the frontline fighter, or a citizen struggling with the political economy, to fight the good fight. The value of *indifference* versus attachment is both social and ethical, guiding one away from material involvement, and metaphysical, pointing to eventual release from the daily round. The twinned antitheses of *elitism* and *egalitarianism* position the actor between two extremes of social structure: where all things are alike, even a warrior and a dog, but where there is also an elite of Brahmins, literal or figurative, who are in the know and stand above the mass. The value of *manliness* in action is enjoined as mandatory; its opposite is the inferior life of weak will and effeminacy, being womanlike, explicitly labeled in the Gita, alluded to at times (albeit qualified) in Thoreau's works. The value of *sacrifice* has many meanings in the Gita, but underlying them is a generic one shared by Thoreau: if all action, especially that dictated by and oriented toward God (Krishna/Nature), is sacrifice, then life itself can be entirely holy. The value of *simplicity*, the conduct of a simple life bared to the essentials, is by both poets counterposed to material excess, luxury, waste, the neglect of spirit. The value of *sincerity*, a truthfulness and honesty in personal relations, is categorically valorized by both poets, while they condemn false show, deceit, and mendacity. The value of *peace* or supreme tranquility, like disinterest, articulates both with a metaphysical level—the total serenity of final liberation—and with things as immediate and practical as living in harmony with your family and your town. Both poets, finally, argue for a life lived in terms of a *complex tension*, praising, on the one hand, purposeful work and right action, while at the same time eloquently advocating partial or occasional retirement and renunciation for the sake of meditation and the pursuit of spiritual values and the intimate signification of the thoughts in great texts. These ten values as roughly defined underlie and order much of the thrust of the argument—or better, persuasiveness—of both the Bhagavad Gita and *Walden*. Let us now consider three of these in more detail: courage/cowardice, sincerity/hypocrisy, and egalitarianism/elitism.

Courage/Cowardice

> And, perceiving your own caste duly,
> You should not tremble.
> Indeed, anything superior to righteous battle
> Does not exist for the Kshatriya [man of warrior
>   caste].
>   (BG, 2.31, Sargeant)

Both poets write, in differing degrees, against a background of war and about the virtue of courage. By "courage," incidentally, I mean not Hemingway's "grace under pressure," nor Frost's "to make the best of what is here and not whine for more," nor Plato's contrast with foolhardiness, but, synthesizing from the Gita and Thoreau, I mean the mettle or moral-psychological backbone to attack or endure an internal or exterior danger, fear, or difficulty.

The Gita is set in a battle; the first line names its field—of *dharma* (duty)—and the rest describes or refers to dozens of times the two main protagonists are situated between the lines of battle. In *Walden* (and his other works) Thoreau is keenly aware of the French and Indian wars and the American Revolution, the latter only sixty years back. The U.S. invasion of Mexico is mentioned several times, notably in the key pages on his arrest for principled tax evasion; Thoreau's consciousness of slavery and his participation in abolitionism, while marginal to *Walden*, were prescient of the Civil War, which was to erupt only six years after the publication of his masterpiece and of which he approved. Both poets evince strong feelings for doing one's duty, as a member of the warrior caste in the case of the Gita:

> If you fail to wage this war
> of sacred duty,
> you will abandon your own duty
> and fame only to gain evil. (2.33, Miller)

In song eighteen, courage and bravery are listed as essential to the second or "passionate" strand of material reality: "Heroism, majesty, firmness, not fleeing in battle . . ." (18.43, Sargeant). There is an unresolved tension in the Gita's positive valorization of "fiery" and other inherent properties of the warrior caste, as contrasted with its negative take on similar passionate traits in other passages. *Walden* and some of Thoreau's essays and lectures laud men such as Oliver Cromwell and John Brown who do their duty fighting for a good cause. Thoreau's concern with "heroism" (like Emerson's), while partly vague indeed and derived from the Latin classics and Thomas Carlyle, is typically concretized in the figures of soldiers, warriors, generals, and Indian fighters (the latter in both senses), whose exemplary martial exploits are at times placed centerstage. For both poets duty is set in the larger context of an abstract courage or bravery that, in turn, is associated with an austere or, for Thoreau, a Spartan way of life (61–62), with simplicity in a Puritan sense.

Courage is typically linked with masculinity and virility (e.g., Latin *virtus*, "manliness, excellence") and is sharply contrasted with effeminacy or femininity and, in the Gita, with impotence. In the Gita the syndrome emerges in many lines, most prominently in songs two and eighteen, which enjoin Arjuna to act the positive and avoid the negative. For example,

> Why this cowardice
> in time of crisis, Arjuna?
> The coward is ignoble, shameful,
> foreign to the ways of heaven. (2.2, Miller)

And, in the next stanza, "Don't yield to impotence! It is unnatural in you!" (2.3, Miller).

Wilkins's eloquent version of the full passage runs: "Whence, O Arjoon, cometh unto thee, thus standing in the field of battle, this folly and unmanly weakness? It is disgraceful, contrary to duty, and the foundation of dishonour. Yield not thus to unmanliness, for it ill becometh one like thee. Abandon this despicable weakness of thy heart, and stand up."

The issue of (Arjuna's) manliness has wider contexts. Arjuna's earlier appearance in the fourth book of the Mahābhārata acting the part of a woman is a subtext for many readers, possibly including Thoreau.[1] In Thoreau's as in Emerson's texts we find occasional expressions of contempt for women and effeminacy, most of which are clichés and all of which need to be balanced by the closeness of both men to leading feminists *avant la lettre* such as Margaret Fuller and Elizabeth Peabody. More salient, however, is Thoreau's praise of courage, primarily physical courage, which often echoes the Gita and indeed the Latin Stoics of which he was so fond. Martial valor and manly courage are in Thoreau but an aspect of the generic courage that begins, pervades, and concludes *Walden.*

Besides the incontrovertible analogies and parallels, there are fundamental differences between the two poets when it comes to courage and cowardice. One difference is that duty for the Gita is grounded in caste—or in whatever euphemism or circumlocution for that structure one prefers. Moreover, in the Gita one reason for acting courageously is the fear of having one's cowardice witnessed: "People will tell of your undying shame, and for a man of honor shame is worse than death," and, in the stanza that follows, "The great chariot warriors will think you deserted in fear of battle; you will be despised by those who held you in esteem" (2.34, 35, Miller). For Thoreau, on the contrary, courage is a virtue that, irrespective of social class, has been internalized by the "heroic" person: a sort of "psychological gyroscope" (Riesman 1950) enables or compels one to act out this inner fortitude with or without an audience. These differences illustrate the well-known antithesis between "shame culture" and "guilt culture." A final difference between the

---

1. This holds, in particular, for many Hindus, including illiterate ones, who, having heard much of the Mahābhārata since childhood, can never read it "for the first time" (Ramanujan 1999, 161); the statement implicitly holds for the Gita, as part of the Mahābhārata. The same could be said of parts of the Bible, some plays of Shakespeare, and parts of Homer for many Westerners.

two poets is that Thoreau often enough mocks, parodies, or criticizes soldiers, battles, and wars, especially when they involve hypocrisy and pride. Yet more overarching than these culturally structured differences is the powerfully suggestive and dialectical tension between the antinomies of act—that is, engagement in right action—versus disengagement from action, particularly action that is evil. The Gita seriatim enjoins "nonviolence" (*ahiṃsā*), also glossed, by Zaehner and others, as "refusal to do harm." The idea of *ahiṃsā* probably affected Thoreau just as it was later to affect Mahatma Gandhi. Yet in songs two and eighteen and at other points Krishna commands, "Fight!" (*yuddh-*), and eventually gives reasons for doing so, immediately on the field of duty, and allegorically in the battle of life. In a similar dualism, Thoreau enjoins civil disobedience by refusing to participate in war, imperialism, slavery and the like, yet also praises not only engagement but necessary war itself, whether of the Roundheads under Cromwell or in the impending struggle against slavery. The dialectic between the thesis of engagement and involvement versus that of disengagement or nonengagement reminds us, incidentally, of the master metaphor of the upside-down tree, which both entangles and protects, and also that of the "sharp ax of detachment," which, with violent engagement, cuts down the tree, but also gives access to tranquility.

Sincerity/Hypocrisy

> Self-conceited, stubborn,
> Filled with pride and the arrogance of wealth,
> They perform sacrifices only in name,
> With hypocrisy, and not according to Vedic injunction.
>   (BG, 16.17, Sargeant)

The idea of hypocrisy (*dambha*), or false display out of self-interest, is a cornerstone of the Gita, where it specifically connotes doing penance, sacrifice, or an austerity, not with the goal of purifying one's soul or of reaching Krishna, but as a façade for actions driven by greed or lust:

Men who practice horrific penances
that go against traditional norms
are trapped in hypocrisy and individuality,
overwhelmed by the emotion of desire. (17.5, Miller)

Here and elsewhere hypocrisy is linked to individualism and the Buddhist triad of desire or lust, anger or hatred, and greed.

Hypocrisy is central to the "demonic" in man: "Hypocrisy, arrogance, overweening pride . . . characterize a man born with demonic traits" (16.4, Edgerton). The sacrifice of such men is for the fruit of action and focused on vain exhibition to gain respect, honor, and reverence (17.12, 18). In the Gita there are fixed or paradigmatic associations, some of which are familiar to us, as in this stanza:

Clinging to insatiable desire,
Filled with hypocrisy, arrogance and pride,
Through delusion taking up false notions,
They proceed with unclean things. (16.10, Edgerton)

The second line of this verse puts hypocrisy and its congeners into a beautiful one-word line: *dambhamānamadānvitāḥ*. A hypocrite of any stripe is thus a mirror image of a man whose falseness faces inward on his innermost self.

Hypocrisy is just as crucial to Thoreau's ethics, figuring centrally in "Economy," and counterposed to integrity, sincerity, and truthfulness. His idea of hypocrisy is contextualized in additional ways: in the hypocrisy of politicians who speechify against slavery while abetting it in their actions; in the hypocrisy of Concord villagers who moralize about chastity while living "sensually"; in the hypocrisy, finally, of philanthropists who give materially without concern for the

souls of their benefactors: "This is a charity that hides a
multitude of sins. The philanthropist too often surrounds
mankind with the remembrance of his own cast-off griefs as
an atmosphere, and calls it sympathy" (52); his underlying
concern is with his "private ail" (53).

The role of hypocrisy in Thoreau obviously draws on
the Hebrew prophets but most of all on Matthew, whose
Christ so often berates foes as "hypocrites."[2] Thoreau's
critique of hypocrisy is counterpointed or contrasted with
unbridled admiration for the denizens of nature, notably
as manifested by loons and foxes, who, although maximally
intelligent, tricksters even, are incapable of hypocrisy.

Egalitarianism/Elitism

Let every one mind his own business, and endeavor
to be what he was made. (*Walden*, 217)

Both poets vacillate between radical egalitarianism and elitism; each can be explicit or devious. The Gita poet in the
second and last songs, in particular, states that caste (*varna*)
is an absolute not to be questioned; breaking castes down
leads to radical mixing and social anomie. Arjuna is told
repeatedly, moreover, to act in terms of his warrior caste
status (one of the seven reasons that he should battle against
his kinsmen in the opposing lines). This is put generally
as well: "Better one's own duty (law, *svadharma*), though
deficient (imperfect), than to perform another's well; better
death in one's own duty (law) than prosperity in another's"
(3.35; see also 18.47, 48).[3] The Gita qualifies deficient per-

---

2. Much of what Thoreau says about hypocrisy and hypocritical charity
more generally has Matthew as one of its sources (e.g., 25.31–46).

3. An important alternative translation to the last clause is "prescribed
by one's own nature," whereas the vulgate reading is "another man's
duty is perilous" (Minor 1982, 137).

formance in the last song with a metaphor: "all undertakings are enveloped in error as a fire is by smoke" (18.48). Caste distinctions between Brahmin, warrior, artisan-merchant, laborer, and even lower levels are assumed in the Gita and related Indian scriptural texts to be inborn, and genetic. What is in fact cultural is seen in these texts as racial and biologically inherited.[4]

Yet the same Gita poet sometimes derogates high-caste ritual, even the Vedas, and, in what sounds to us like a Dostoievskian flourish, advocates the *yoga* of devotion (*bhakti*), which makes salvation through Lord Krishna open to us all: "Even a hardened criminal, if he worships (loves) me alone, is to be thought of as a saint (virtuous man), for he has indeed resolved matters correctly" (9.30), and then, "Even those born from evil wombs (i.e., of low caste origin), Arjuna, women, men of the merchant class (*vaiśyas*) or of the fourth (and lowest) caste (*śūdras*), if they rely on me (take shelter in me) will travel the highest way" (9.32). Through two millennia, then, the Gita has functioned both as a charter for caste (and has been so perceived by many individuals of lower-caste origin; see, e.g., Deepankar 2000), *but also* as an ideology of social leveling by revolutionaries such as Mahatma Gandhi (Desai 1951), who studied and quoted from the Gita while leading the national struggle for Indian liberation from the oppressive and pernicious institutions of caste and colonialism (see chapter 9). Be it noted there are many points in the Vedas and the (Vedic) Upanishads that say that the way to God or the Supreme Being is open to those who have only faith (e.g., Roy 1832, 20); the passage in Roy about only eating meat in "the time

---

4. This confusion underlies the thinking of many in America today; in the same vein I am using the politically incorrect word "caste" for social stratification that is relatively absolute in terms of language, lifestyle, prohibitions against marriage, residence, profession, and so forth. Chicago in many parts and to a significant degree also has caste-like social boundaries.

of distress" cited in *Walden* (146) is the same as that made in the Katha Upanishad 1.26.

Reading the Gita probably reinforced Thoreau's ambivalence and division of mind about the ethics of social stratification. On the one hand, he often seems to be in at least implicit collusion with the local ethnic structure of Old American Yankee "Brahmins," Native Americans, and Irish, or, financially speaking, old money, (indebted) farmers, the village poor, and merchants and artisans such as his pencil-making father—or himself, the surveyor. In what sounds like an adaptation of Gita 3.35 above, Thoreau writes, "Let every one mind his own business, and endeavor to be what he was made . . . If a man does not keep pace with his companions, perhaps it is because he hears a different drummer"; so that, if you are a pygmy, you will at least be "the biggest pygmy that [you] can." Here Thoreau's wording is relatively close to the original. Wilkins's translation runs: "A man's own religion, though contrary to, is better than the faith of another, be it ever so well followed" ([1785] 1959, 48–49); Wilkins's "religion" and "faith" and his rhetoric of dissent *may* have spoken more directly to Thoreau's Puritan sensibilities. Finally, the "once-and-a-half witted" need not "level downward to our dullest perceptions" (217).

Thoreau's sense of class and caste was reinforced by several kinds of elitism in which he participated and which inform some of his writings. First, the idea of an elect few is widespread in the New Testament, notably in the First Evangelist, Matthew (e.g., the parable of the tares in chapter 13). Another kind of elitism informs some of the Pauline Epistles, notably Corinthians, which Thoreau seems to have internalized early on.[5] Calvinist elitism, finally, was

---

5. This idea occurs in St. Paul in 2 Corinthians 6.7, the Gita 3.35 and 18.4, and *Walden*: if he is a pygmy, he will at least be "the biggest pygmy that he can" (217) resembles 1 Corinthians 7.20, "Let every man abide in the same calling wherein he was called."

endemic in his native Concord. A second kind of elitism that fed into Thoreau was the idea of a select few, mainly poets and "seers," who can see and understand Nature and sacred scriptures. This latter kind of elitism looms large in Emerson, European Romanticism, and indeed much of the medieval and classical poetry that Thoreau was so fond of—and in the Gita and the Rig Veda.

Yet as with the Gita, Thoreau at other points is signally egalitarian in spirit and in practice—for example, in choosing a locale of down-and-outers and ex-slaves by Walden Pond, as described in detail in "Former Inhabitants," in appreciating the *Men of Concord* of all walks of life (as anthologized in Allen 1936), and in seeing that everyone has some special gift: "It is a pleasant fact that you will know no man long however low in the social scale[,] however poor[,] miserable, intemperate & worthless he may appear to be[,] a mere burden to society—but you will find at last that there is something which he understands & can do better than any other" (*Journal* 1850; Rossi 285). Or, in *Walden*:

> I desire that there may be as many different persons in the world as possible; but I would have each one be very careful to find out and pursue *his own* way, and not his father's or his mother's or his neighbor's instead. The youth may build or plant or sail, only let him not be hindered from doing that which he tells me he would like to do. It is by a mathematical point only that we are wise, as the sailor or the fugitive slave keeps the polestar in his eye; but that is sufficient guidance for all our life. We may not arrive at our port within a calculable period, but we would preserve the true course. (48)

At a less idealistic level, Thoreau's egalitarian side and propensities show up at numerous places in his other writings, most dramatically and convincingly in his full portrait of Joe Polis, his Algonquin friend and the guide during a hunting party in the Maine woods (Thoreau 1988). Not only does he start to learn Joe's language but he competes with him physically in a comradely and egalitarian fashion. Thoreau's Joe Polis matches the best of portraits by top-notch professional anthropologists (Casagrande 1960); the way he treats him as an equal, and not as an "informant" giving information to a social scientist, would seem to block a colonialist reading.

Thoreau's belief in the common man was nourished by his likewise strongly held belief in individual skill or craft—of a woodchopper, hunters, and fishermen, with their knowledge gained through the experience of practice. Thoreau saw the great potential or possible future in every man, including a "cone-headed" Irish infant that would and could some day acquire winged *sandalia*, that is, the winged sandals of knowledge, and so rise up in the world (140). His egalitarianism was consistent with his political anarchism or, better, anarcho-syndicalism, where a rebel attitude toward tyranny or any wrongdoing by any state was woven together with a desire to be a good citizen of one's local community, a good Concordian. Thoreau has in fact been coupled with Emerson and Whitman as one of the most eloquent advocates of "the new belief (or image) of the common man" (C. Friedrich 1950). There is in Thoreau, finally, a strong element of the Jeffersonian ideology to which he was heir, where the virtues of industry, self-reliance, and acquired knowledge were open to all "natural aristocrats" and could facilitate the upward mobility that his own life illustrated—not forgetting, as Thoreau probably did not, that Jefferson's "all men are created equal" and the like coexisted with practices that reinforced slaveholding (Wills 2003). Thoreau's egalitarianism was actually vastly more radical than Jefferson's. Thoreau's many expressions here and elsewhere of the unique abilities, even genius, in every man, are reminiscent of Baudelaire's claim that "In Balzac even the concierge is a man of genius." This also, however, like Jefferson's "natural aristocrat," constitutes a sort of middle ground between elitism and egalitarianism that is consistent with his argument for a middle path in general.

To conclude this section, the dialectic, explicit or implicit, between anarchic egalitarianism and Brahmanical elitism constitutes a powerful common denominator between and within the two texts that is never resolved despite artful elaborations. One fact of life about scriptural writings, including the Bible and the Koran, is that, as already noted, they often articulate contradictions without resolving them and have served to justify diametrically opposed activities.

.

Chapter Six

Purity

What sort of life would result if we had attained to purity? . . . Man flows at once to God when the channel of purity is open.

—Henry David Thoreau, *Walden*

The pivotal workings of the value of purity in the thought of both poets is instantiated by powerful figuration. Its workings as a pivot are also exemplified by its double, Janus-faced status and function. On the one hand, it clearly belongs to the set of social and ethical categories introduced in the last chapter because, for example, it both enjoins one to bathe at dawn and to avoid the delusions of the soul. On the other hand, purity is associated with the divine, interacting with essence and other ontological categories to be dealt with further on.

Purity, while perhaps more complex than any other absolute, also brings together the two poets. Purity is one of the deepest values in the Gita; in the Sanskrit there are several near-synonymous terms such as *sauca-* or *suci-*, and *uddha-*, and purity is related to allied terms with associated meanings of merit and value such as *punya-* and the productive root for "(to) clean": *pu-*. The value of purity is never questioned or parodied. Its meanings are revealed by many contexts, by the way they radiate out to the meanings of other values. Negatively defined, it is opposed to and contrasted with the general idea of sin and evil (*pāpa-*), and many other components of the third "strand," notably indolence and slothfulness (e.g., 14.8), and delusion or illusion, which latter (*moha*) one mighty commentator also glossed as "error, perverseness, hallucination" (14.13; Rāmānuja in Minor 1982, 410). Speaking positively, good fruit results from pure and untainted conduct, as when one acts without involvement: "Disinterested, pure (of the defilement of passion), renouncing all undertakings" (12.16). One crucial kind of purity is cleanliness, be it the bodily cleanliness from bathing, or the cleanliness of one's inner self, or of a lotus flower. Equally concrete is the literal chastity of a priest, who not only performs sacrifice, and honors gods, priests, teachers, and wise men, but exemplifies celibacy, uprightness, and non-violence (17.14)—with irony here, since Brahmins are often not celibate, or even chaste; elsewhere on the Indian scene procreation by adult Brahmins is emphatically enjoined.

At a higher level purity is akin to practices of austerity (*tapas*) and discipline (*yoga*): "As he sits on his seat, let him pinpoint his mind, so that the workings of mind and sense are under control, and yoke himself to yoga for the cleansing of himself" (6.12, van Buitenen), until he is "purified by the fire of knowledge" (4.10). Gita purity, to repeat, is a component of the highest "strand" of the three nature-given types or categories on which the whole poem pivots and the definition of which in terms of no less than fourteen variables brings it to its ultimate climax in songs seventeen and eighteen. Gita purity is part of the ultimate value of devotion or love (*bhakti*) of the divine. Gita purity is a component of perfection and of the perfect, highest state.

The value of purity, with its obvious sources in the Christian tradition, including medieval literature, was also one of the absolutes in the template of Thoreau's mind, something of which he was keenly, even self-consciously aware. It was reinforced by readings of the Gita when it came to such categories as physical cleanliness, personal chastity, and a simple life linked to "simplicity, independence, magnanimity, and trust" (9), and faith. Yet purity in Thoreau, in a departure from the Gita and its lotus, is also thought of in terms of wild animals, all of whom are pure and some of whom, such as the loon, are idealized, even idolized conspicuously. It is also thought of as the crystalline and kaleidoscopic chromaticity of Walden Pond, and simply as the blue part of the spectrum: the color blue and its cousins occur many times in relation to Walden, sometimes "more cerulean than the sky itself" (119), and blue is "evidence of its purity" (217).

Diverse connotations of purity may bunch together to intensify its values, as when the word and its derivations dominate whole paragraphs. They occur no less than ten times in one one-and-a-half page stretch (147–48), where they spoke out in many directions, to chastity and cleanliness, even to touching the jawbone of a dead hog that Thoreau found in the woods. Critical here and identical to the Gita is this: "All sensuality is one, though it takes many forms; all purity is one. It is the same whether a man eat, or drink, or cohabit, or sleep sensually. They are but one appetite, and we only need to see a person do any one of these things to know how great a sensualist he is" (147–48; "sensual" for Thoreau usually means "sexual"). Thoreau's ideas of purity are further adumbrated and complicated when, with typical double-mindedness, he admits to finding *Leaves of Grass* "exhilarating, encouraging" and also to his own impurity (Hindus 1971, 67–68).[1] In sum, purity in

---

1. The fascinating relation between Thoreau and Whitman is partly clarified by the following: "There are two or three pieces in this book which are disagreeable, to say the least: simply sensual. He does not celebrate love at all. It is as if the beasts spoke. I think that men have not been ashamed of themselves without reason. No doubt there have always been dens where such deeds were unblushingly recited, and it is no merit to compete with their inhabitants. But even on this side he has shown more truth than any American or Modern that I know. I found his poem exhilarating, encouraging. As for its sensuality,—and it may turn out to be less sensual than it appears,—I do not so much wish those parts were not written, as that men and women were so pure that they could read them without harm, that is, without understanding them" (in Hindus 1971, 67–68).

Thoreau differs sufficiently from his Christian, particularly
Puritan heritage that one is inclined to think that he owes
much to the Gita and, specifically, its *sattvik* connotations
of fire, light, knowledge, and lucidity and, negatively, its
opposition to ignorance and slothfulness (granted William
Langland and similar writers could have influenced him
here).

A decisive aspect of the problem of purity is the way
in both poets it is essential to perfection. Perfection and
purity, be it noted right off, overlap but are not identical:
gold is pure when without alloy or admixture, whereas a
rose is perfect in terms of some explicit or implicit model.
The idea of perfection (*siddhi*) occurs throughout the Gita,
often as the end for which purity is the means; at one point,
Arjuna asks if a man of faith but lacking ascetic discipline
and one "who does not attain perfection in yoga will be lost
like a disappearing cloud, having fallen from both worlds,
having no solid ground, confused on the path of Brahman"
(6.38, Sargeant), to which Krishna replies that "the man
of discipline, purified of his sins, perfected through many
births, finds the higher way" (6.45, Miller). In Thoreau's
case we have the climactic parable near the end of *Walden*
of the artist of Kouroo, who took eons to make a staff from
which new worlds flowed: "The material was pure, and his
art was pure; how could the result be other than wonderful?" (218)—that is, perfect.[2] The parable deserves to be
cited in full, as follows:

> There was an artist in the city of Kouroo who was
> disposed to strive after perfection. One day it came
> into his mind to make a staff. Having considered

---

2. The parable of the artist of Kouroo with its Indian nuances was
probably invented by Thoreau—in the sense that no convincing source
for it has been found so far among the three main candidates (Hodder
2001, 330).

that in an imperfect work time is an ingredient,
but into a perfect work time does not enter, he
said to himself, It shall be perfect in all respects,
though I should do nothing else in my life. He
proceeded instantly to the forest for wood, being
resolved that it should not be made of unsuitable
material; and as he searched for and rejected stick
after stick, his friends gradually deserted him, for
they grew old in their works and died, but he grew
not older by a moment. His singleness of purpose
and resolution, and his elevated piety, endowed
him, without his knowledge, with perennial youth.
As he made no compromise with Time, Time
kept out of his way, and only sighed at a distance
because he could not overcome him. Before he
had found a stock in all respects suitable the city
of Kouroo was a hoary ruin, and he sat on one of
its mounds to peel the stick. Before he had given
it the proper shape the dynasty of the Candahars
was at an end, and with the point of the stick he
wrote the name of the last of that race in the
sand, and then resumed his work. By the time he
had smoothed and polished the staff Kalpa was
no longer the pole-star; and ere he had put on
the ferule and the head adorned with precious
stones, Brahma had awoke and slumbered many
times. But why do I stay to mention these things?
When the finishing stroke was put to his work, it
suddenly expanded before the eyes of the astonished artist into the fairest of all the creations of
Brahma. He had made a new system in making
a staff, a world with full and fair proportions; in
which, though the old cities and dynasties had
passed away, fairer and more glorious ones had
taken their places. And now he saw by the heap
of shavings still fresh at his feet, that, for him

and his work, the former lapse of time had been an illusion, and that no more time had elapsed than is required for a single scintillation from the brain of Brahma to fall on and inflame the tinder of a mortal brain. The material was pure, and his art was pure; how could the result be other than wonderful? (218)

The perfectness of the staff is clearly if implicitly reticulated with the network of ax/axis symbolism elsewhere in *Walden*.

Let us push deeper on the symbolism of purity. The lotus, a symbol of purity in the Gita and other Indian classics that Thoreau was absorbing, recurs at key points throughout his work—as a lily. A remarkable passage ten pages into *A Week on the Concord and Merrimac Rivers* climaxes its listing of ten riverine flowers (and their ten colors) with the water lily:

> But we missed the white water-lily, which is the queen of river flowers, its reign being over for this season. He makes his voyage too late, perhaps, by a true water clock who delays so long. Many of this species inhabit our Concord water. I have passed down the river before sunrise on a summer morning between fields of lilies still shut in sleep; and when, at length, the flakes of sunlight from over the bank fell on the surface of the water, whole fields of white blossoms seemed to flash open before me, as I floated along, like the unfolding of a banner, so sensible is this flower to the influence of the sun's rays. ("Saturday"; 1980, 10)

(That it was missing then, it being September, illustrates the author's figure of the missing signified.) Yet more conclusive: on the last page of "Slavery in Massachusetts" Thoreau finds the first water lily of spring, ". . . the emblem of purity . . . It suggests what kind of laws have prevailed longest and widest" (2002, 193). Not limited by the Gita's poetic compression, Thoreau spells out the analogy as an allegory: the lily is purity, courage, and sweetness in human affairs, whereas the slime and muck underneath stand for the hypocrisy and immorality of local and national politics (see Buell 1989, 6–29, for a diametrically opposed take on this passage).

A sifting through and inspection of the pertinent passages has carried us further into the aforementioned complexity, and has also suggested problems of potential irony. On the one hand, purity as an absolute ideal is not seriously questioned. On the other hand, when it comes to purity as lived out in practice, knowledge, and even faith (and *bhakti*), there is a recognition, widely distinguished and wisely discerned by both poets, of actual, underlying, ineradicable human impurity. Thoreau admits to his own impurity at various points—"I never knew, and never shall know, a worse man than myself" (53). We saw this earlier when discussing his opinion of Whitman. Actual human impurity is referred to or alluded to many times in the Gita. Some readers, *not* including myself, would claim that both poets are implicitly calling purity into question (Bartscherer 2004). Ironies, ambivalences, and contradictions are, in any case, distilled in many ways: both the lotus and the lily stand for ideal purity or, better, the ideal of purity, yet the former flower grows in and is "washed" by the River Ganges with its human filth just as the latter grows amid the muck and duckweed of the Concord River.

Which brings us to a terminal contrast and complementation. The respective (key) words and idioms recall the initial dichotomy of practicality versus metaphysics and the conclusion that here too there is much in common between the two poets. For both, purity can be achieved or at least striven for through the avoidance of or cleansing from sloth, filth, sensuality, lust, evil. Thoreau, bespeaking his partly Christian ethics ("in-nocence," the "im-maculate" conception, and so forth), would seem to mean such purity through avoidance more than does the Gita poet, yet the latter also says much about getting oneself cleansed of corruption, and foul or passion-bred habits. The second purity, to continue, is the essential kind, emanating from within; it is the divine within all things, including turtles and loons, that draws from and reflects universal cosmic purity. Thoreau's idea of purity specifically stems from the intensely local tradition of Puritanism. Second, his purity is global or universal because it reflects formal perfection in a classic (Platonic or Pythagorean) sense, be it that of a mathematical demonstration such as his own in "The Pond in Winter" or the perfect pitch of the hermit thrush and indeed most songbirds. Both poets, finally, predicate much of their argument, or urge their position, on this second purity within cerulean water, fiery heat, and the upright man, yet they do not neglect the contributory role of, for instance, external rituals of diet.

Chapter Seven

Reality and Being

We think that that *is* which *appears* to be.

—Bhagavad Gita, 65

I am time/death (*kāla*).

—Bhagavad Gita, 10.30

The fundamental premise in the ontologies of both poets is the reality of the essence within matter, and the ubiquity of it—not "essence" in our Western sense of the minimal, indispensable, or characteristic, but as a vital spark, a bit of life, something dynamic, a spiritus. No matter what is at stake, be it water or horses, whores, huckleberries or Walden Pond, it has an essence in this sense. The essence of all things knowable or beyond knowledge can be alluded to or given intimations of in an infinity of ways, particularly the linguistic ones so brilliantly exemplified by both poets: when Krishna, for example, says, "I am the flavor[1] of water" (7.8), he means that he is a metaphor of that flavor and the flavor itself is a synecdoche for the water's inner life. Amid the ubiquity of essence, two kinds above all are to be assumed.

---

1. The quality in question has also been variously glossed as "liquidity," "fragrance," and "taste."

Every individual, be it an elephant or a fox, but, most relevantly, every human being, houses within a material vessel an individual spirit or soul that, like a psychic double or other Self, will eventually pass into another body bearing some trace or fragrance of its earlier bodies along with it. The whole universe, in the second place, is inhabited by a universal essence or cosmic oversoul in which the individual Selves participate and which is active in them without being influenced by them. As against the fundamental reality of essence—the *is* beneath the *seems*, which is true meaning—there stretches—indeed roils—a vast network or grid of falseness and delusion structured by false and sinful dichotomies or opposites of word, deed, or thought in terms of which human beings act and feel and think. To be free of this delusion, be it enslavement in the political economy or the dark inertia of lower-class ignorance, is or should be the primary goal. It can be achieved by work, knowledge, and devotion to God in the form of Nature or Krishna. Through this God one may gain resurrection and redemption from the endless, grinding round of life.[2] The most fundamental reality of this God is infinite extension in time and space, which we can never grasp and by which we are or will be absorbed. To illustrate and validate this shared ontology, here grossly oversimplified, let us turn to an empirical, philological analysis of the total field of metaphysical absolutes under six rubrics: body and self, matter and the levels of spirit, essence, the denial of opposites, liberation from delusion (*dvandva-moha-nir-mukta*), and the infinitudes.

Body and Self/Spirit

We are so degraded that we cannot speak simply of the necessary functions of human nature. (*Walden*, 148)

---

2. While *moksha* or liberation is the closure of continual existence as we understand it, it is similar to the Christian idea of salvation from sin; resurrection in Thoreau is complexly related to but critically different from Christian redemption, a contrast that calls for further analysis.

Our poets have similar attitudes toward the body as at once sacred and profane. The Gita speaks of our nine orifices as follows: "Having renounced all actions with the mind, the embodied soul dwells happily, the master, in its nine-gated city (citadel), neither acting at all nor causing to act" (5.13). Like the Laws of Manu, the Gita deals with the body's functions in a way that we would call naturalistic, putting eating, drinking, sleeping, having sex, urinating, breathing, and so forth, on the same line. Many passages evince a concern with maintaining bodily purity through diet and ritual, and inveigh against mortification or any desecration of the flesh (see chapter 6, "Purity," and, in chapter 8). Yet for the Gita poet this same body is but a material wrap: "As leaving aside worn-out bodies / To other, new ones goes the embodied soul" (2.22, Edgerton).

Thoreau speaks similarly of the body: "Every man is the builder of a temple, called his body, to the god he worships, after a style purely his own, nor can he get off by hammering marble instead" (148).[3] He enjoins care of this temple through swimming at dawn, avoidance of coffee, and other semi-ritualized practices—these practices contradict the Gita in that they have the goal of heightening one's awareness to what the Indian calls "the objects of sense."[4] Thoreau emphatically approves of the Hindu naturalism that treats of the body and its physiology with a lack of shame that contrasts with Puritan taboos to which he was subject: "Nothing was too trivial for the Hindoo lawgiver, however

---

3. St. Paul's words on the body, part of Thoreau's background and deep memory, sensitized him to the Gita: 1 Corinthians, for example, goes, "What! Know ye not that your body is the temple of the Holy Ghost, which is in you . . . ?" (6.20), and, "therefore glorify the Lord in your body, and in your spirit, which are God's" (6.20). See also 3.16.

4. The one apparent or partial exception occurs in 15.9: "Hearing, sight, and touch, / and taste and smell, / making use of (or presiding over) these and the thought-organ (*manas*), he (i.e., the fragment of the Lord incarnated as the individual soul) / devotes himself to the objects of sense." As Minor (1982, 424) has also pointed out, this stanza includes *manas*, the organ that is directly involved in perception, but does *not* include *buddhi* (higher) intelligence (nor *ahaṁkāra*, the "I-doer").

offensive it may be to modern taste. He teaches how to eat, drink, cohabit, void excrement and urine, and the like, elevating what is mean, and does not falsely excuse himself by calling these things trifles" (148). Like the Gita poet, Thoreau equates the various sensuous needs and desires as in the sentence already cited: "It is the same whether a man eat, or drink, or cohabit, or sleep sensually. They are but one appetite" (147).

The two poets differ, however, on metempsychosis. The Gita is definite, even repetitious, about the passing of the Self (*ātman*) from one body to another through time, whereas for Thoreau this was, as noted elsewhere, only or mainly an intriguing, indeed fascinating, possibility that he implies or uses as a metaphysical trope. The characters in his "Brute Neighbors" or "Winter Animals" chapters, for example, can be read as metaphors of human stereotypes, or as fauna inhabited by souls with a human past.[5] The human body, in any case, is a temporary dwelling from which the spirit will pass: "When the play, it may be the tragedy, of life is over, the spectator goes his way" (91). Dhawan (1985, 78), on the other hand, forthrightly claims that, "Thoreau seems to have a firm conviction in the Hindu doctrine of transmigration and immortality of the soul. The several references to this theory, in the letters and journals, do reveal his belief in the continuity of life."

The intensity of Thoreau's debt to Hindu corporeality would seem to motivate a fascinating and intricate etymology. At one point in his journal (26 December 1841), he wrote, "The whole duty of life is contained in this question How to respire and aspire both at once." At one level this alludes to the twin realms of the bodily and the ethereal,

---

5. One model for this would be the *Harivamsa* tale about souls passing between ducks and sages that Thoreau (1932) translated from a French translation while he was working on *Walden*. The fuller statement on spirit occurs in the next section in this chapter, "Matter and the Levels of Spirit."

the wild and the spiritual. At a second level it is yet another bit of Thoreau's exuberant Latinate wordplay in the often almost bilingual texts of this author, since *re-spirare* means "to draw in one's breath, inhale," while *a-spirare* means "to exhale." At a deeper level within this Latinism both verbs derive from *spiritus*, "breath" or "spirit," which can have not just spiritual but corporeal meanings (e.g., "spirit" can mean semen or sperm in Shakespeare; Jakobson 1987, 201–202). Going sideways, as it were, these Latinate intricacies connect with two important meanings in the Indic literature on rules for ritual: "Others sacrifice by suspending the cycle of vital breath, the flow of inhaling (*prāna*) and exhaling (*apānam*), as they practice breath control" (4.29, Miller; see also 5.27 and 15.14). (The more complicated Wilkins translation runs: "Some there are who sacrifice their breathing spirit, and force it downwards from its natural course; whilst others force the spirit which is below back with the breath; and a few, with whom these faculties are held in great esteem, close up the door of each" ([1785] 1959, 54–55).) Thus from the abstract vision of the body as a microcosm, to the physical specifics of bodily function and ritual, Thoreau's attitude owes much to Indian carnality and corporeality. What he says about breathing may also reflect his or Emerson's study of Plato's *Timaeus* (1920, 56).

Matter and the Levels of Spirit

At a metaphysical level our poets see being and reality similarly. Gita poetry, to begin, is predicated on a fundamental, repetitiously reiterated and deceptive dualism. On the one hand, there is the manifest and transient world. We learn something of its content, for example, from the dozens of references to the body and its functions. We get further inklings not through empirical descriptions but from the allusions in metaphors, metonyms, and other figures: sod, elephant, turtle, fire, smoke, mirror, blood. We also get inklings from the hundreds of ways Krishna is defined: lightning among wind gods, the sacred fig tree, the immortal stallion, the powers of fame, fortune, speech, memory, intelligence, resolve, and patience (all feminine, as already noted, by virtue of the gender of the respective nouns). At this level matter includes the mind and, as noted, phenomena that in modern Western thought are usually classified as psychological or mental: "My (material) nature is divided eightfold: earth, water, fire, wind, space (or ether), mind, understanding (or intelligence), and individuality (or self-consciousness; literally the "I-maker," *ahaṁkāra*)" (7.4). It also includes things that we would classify as cultural as against natural: the castes and the three strands or dimensions of nature—roughly, enlightenment or lucidity, passion, and, in Miller's happy gloss, dark inertia, that is, ignorance and slothfulness; as these glosses imply, the degree and type of light is one of the sharpest definers of spirit (see "Eye and Light," in chapter 4). The three material strands braid together to make the rope that binds man to the material world.

Contrasting with the manifest world is the innermost individual spirit of a man (*ātman*), which, when transmigrating, leaves the body behind like an old suit of clothes (2.22). Second is the general spirit of man (*purusha*). Beyond these spirits are the many levels of the supreme or cosmic spirit (Brahman). This macrocosmic spirit or oversoul participates in each individual microcosmic spirit just as each of the latter is part of the former. The interplay between the indwelling spirit and its material vessel is lost in most translations but does come through intelligibly when the inner self is capitalized and opposed to the minuscule (which is usually the reflexive form), as in the excellent version by Sargeant:

> One should uplift oneself by the Self;
> One should not degrade oneself;

For the Self alone can be a friend to oneself,
And the Self alone can be the enemy of oneself.

For him who has conquered himself by the Self,
The Self is a friend;
But for him who has not conquered himself,
The Self remains hostile, like an enemy.[6] (6.5–6)

The Wilkins interpretation goes as follows: "He should raise himself by himself: he should not suffer his soul to be depressed. Self is the friend of self; and in like manner, self is its own enemy. Self is the friend of him by whom the spirit is subdued with the spirit; so self, like a foe, delighteth in the enmity of him who hath no soul" ([1785] 1959, 62–63).

The division between the inner spirit and its material vessel, between Self and the self, is not absolute or categorical, however. Consistent with its general openness, the Gita, on the one hand, allows that some "fragrance" of the material body may adhere to the transmigrating soul as it moves out like the wind: "the master who takes on a body and again escapes it, transmigrating out of it with these senses as the wind moves on with the scents it has taken from their sources" (15.8, van Buitenen). On the other hand, the world spirit or oversoul is at times like a wind within space, at other times like the space itself within which the winds of all the other entities are blown about.

The many kinds of reality, material and spiritual, are encompassed and contained by the one Krishna who, both the seed and the womb (14.3–4), generates all and consumes all things—unless they break free from the cycle of life. The cosmic, totalizing One can be approached through knowledge and right action, and reached by faith, as is dealt with in chapter 1.

---

6. This categorical distinction between the self and the Self *may* also be seen as "a translator's stop-gap solution to what is deliberately obtuse and polysemic on the part of the *Gita* poet" (Cox, Whitney, 2004. Personal communication).

Thoreau's levels of reality, together with obvious debts to Goethe and others, reflect a deep internalization of the Gita and of Emerson's reading of it. To begin, *Walden* is grounded in the empirical reality of local fauna and flora, and with the landscapes which are so masterfully represented and with which Thoreau interacted so multifariously; he was, after all, a fisherman and master surveyor, and for two years a tiller of the soil. Yet any of these Thoreauvian realia, while seemingly objective and in some sense realistic, can at any time turn out to be just as symbolic as the Gita's turtle. In other words, Thoreau's exact, natural scientific observations of sumac and loon go hand-in-glove with the symbolic. Neither gains supremacy; rather, they are inseparable. The symbolic power of nature observed derives from the empirical reality of it, and that reality is underwritten by the symbolic. But let us go deeper.

Thoreau's "Realometer" measures beyond the empirical: you cut and scrape downward to the rocky bottom—or the closest you can get to it—where the fact may cut through you like a cimeter (or an ax), but you can also move outwards into realms beyond the eyes of the partridge in your hand or the somnolent owl during the day when you're staring at it or the "silly" loon who outwits you: beyond all these is the intelligence or "civilization" of Nature. Beyond this or governing it from within are the principles or laws, the harmonies or processes of Nature that can be suggested and illustrated by a sandbank thawing in spring. Still further beyond stretch supernal realms, corresponding to the Gita's "unmanifest behind the unmanifest" (8.20–22), of which we get intimations from the iridescence of a lake's surface or the play of light from a rainbow, or on a pickerel.

Thoreau's ideas of the self parallel those of the Gita, although couched differently. The oversoul is of course Nature, but unlike Emerson's version and like the Gita's, this macrocosm includes the bad and the good, the cruel and the benign, the destructive as well as the creative, death as well as birth. The soul of the individual, corresponding to the Gita's *ātman*, partakes of the oversoul and vice versa. The eternal souls move about from one empirical or experiential body to another as a body moves from one suit of clothes to another (15). Numerous passages in *Walden*, sometimes whole chapters, such as "Brute Neighbors" and "Winter Animals," make fuller sense if we assume not only metaphorical or allegorical similitudes but the transmigrations, if only as a trope, between and among the souls of Thoreau and his fellow Concordians and the animals whom he depicts with such memorable vividness. A natural historian's exactitude here blocks a sentimental anthropomorphism while it makes credible or at least easily imaginable that a person was, could be, or will eventually inhabit a woodchuck, a red ant, or a loon. Thoreau's soul or self, like the Gita's, is double in nature—one empirical, experiential, and material, the other spiritual; between these two selves there is "a perpetual nextness" (Cavell 1981, 108):

> However intense my experience, I am conscious
> of the presence and criticism of a part of me,
> which, as it were, is not a part of me, but spectator,
> sharing no experience, but taking note of it; and
> that is no more I than it is you. When the play, it
> may be the tragedy, of life is over, the spectator
> goes his way. (91)

Essence and Tropology: Synecdoche and the Punch of Cumulative, Climactic, Terminal Metaphor

"I am the taste in water," says Krishna in the seventh song, exemplifying a complex semiotics of essence. In fact, both poets assume, as indispensable, that everything has an essence, meaning, as already noted here, not a defining attribute, but an inherent, necessary, and deeper gist or inward nature, the inner seed. Not only do they assume this, they essentialize promiscuously in two ways that have been called the master tropes in poetics and language: metaphor and synecdoche.

To begin by recurring to a fuller gloss of the line just quoted above, both define essence as part of a whole: "I am the taste/flavor/liquidity of water" is but the first and perhaps most striking synecdoche in a long string that includes "the understanding of a wife" and "the strength of the strong free from desire and passion" (7.11). Here are three stanzas in full, putting "the taste in water" in context:

> I am taste in water, son of Kuntī,
>   I am light in the moon and sun,
> The sacred syllable (*om*) in all the Vedas,
>   Sound in ether, manliness in men.

> Both the goodly odor in earth,
>   And brilliance in fire am I,
> Life in all beings,
>   And austerity in ascetics am I.

> The seed of all beings am I,
>   The eternal, be assured, son of Prthā;
> I am intelligence of the intelligent,
>   Majesty of the majestic am I. (7.8–10, Edgerton)

The many synecdochic essences in *Walden* run from the howl of a loon to the fragrance of freshly picked huckleberries: "The ambrosial and essential part of the fruit is lost with the bloom which is rubbed off in the market cart" (117). The maximum of something is of course one variant of this kind of essence: the maximum evil of slavery, the maximum beauty of autumnal tints for Thoreau; whereas the Gita poet sings, "I am the cosmic serpent," "the syllable OM," and so forth (10.29, 25). Yet another variant of this kind transcends opposites: "I am immortality and death; both being and non-being" (9.19). That a phenomenon may have many such essences is instanced by Walden Pond itself: its mist, its echoes, its nymphs, and its colors in the bluish-green, glaucous parts of the spectrum.

The list, particularly those in the form of an extended inventory of synecdoches, is in fact a sterling common denominator of these two works. Extended inventories of five, ten, and even dozens of items occur throughout the Gita and Thoreau. They may function as the core of a book. The great epiphany of Krishna in book eleven takes us intermittently from "hundreds and thousands" of shapes and colors to many mouths and aspects, to arms, bellies, and tusks, to yet more gods (39)—one hundred items or more, depending on how we count. Sometimes the climax is in the center of the list: "Of a thousand suns in the sky / If suddenly should burst forth / The light, it would be like / Unto the light of the exalted one"[7] (11.12, Edgerton).

Extended inventories jut out equally in Thoreau's rhetoric, notably of flora: berries, flowers, and trees. Midway through the "Sounds" chapter comes a list of nine plants, mainly berries, that is climaxed by a marvelous paragraph on the sumac in August, whose "large masses of berries, which, when in flower, had attracted many wild bees, gradually assumed their bright velvety crimson hue, and by their weight again bent down and broke the tender limbs" (77). But this penchant for inventories goes deeper: many of the chapters are so structured, not only "Sounds," but "The Ponds," "Brute Neighbors," "Former Inhabitants," and "Winter Visitors" and "Winter Animals." As in the Gita, some of these lists are open-ended and suggest the infinite while others are signally turned off: "The Ponds" by the upside-down tree, and "Brute Neighbors" by the loon, his mythic

---

7. Which passage occurred to physicist Robert Oppenheimer when he saw the first atomic explosion in the deserts of New Mexico.

grandeur counterpoised against Thoreau's ornithological precision. By permissive standards, about half the chapters in *Walden* are built on lists, so much so that the book, like Whitman's *Leaves of Grass*, approximates a list of lists. Going outside *Walden*, the "autumnal tints" in his essay of that name (2002, 215–43) are a symbol for (and celebration of) death by means of a procession of trees in their autumn glory—notably the oaks and maples, just as the lily is the ultimate flower and the huckleberry the berry of berries. All this is seen as a weakness by thinkers who value deductive, hierarchical thought while eschewing the great associative power of the list.

The power of such synecdochic essentializing connects both Thoreau and the Gita to the larger issue of catalogue and sacred numbers—"The Sacred Seven" of Emerson's celebrated "Brahma" poem or the seventy names of God (Izmirlieva 2000, 6–7, 54–56). By recounting all the members of a set rather than alluding to them metaphorically, a sense of totality is achieved. Be it a list of ten berries or one hundred attributes of Lord Krishna, the inventory has the power of a synecdoche—or better, a metonym—that is, of units contiguous in time, space, kind, or origin (Jakobson 1987, 109–14). But the same extended inventory, when its members are grouped together because of a shared feature or even a vague similarity, as in these two examples, also has the power of a complex metaphor. The fact that the list is both metaphoric and metonymic, and the way the extended list strengthens both these tropes, gives rhetorical power to both the Gita and Thoreau (and to many religious texts of the world). The extended inventory works synergistically with the climactic metaphor, to which I return below.[8] The

---

8. The list in North America has been discussed by Buell, who treats of Thoreau's friends, Channing and Alcott, but focuses on Emerson and Thoreau. Buell calls it that aspect of Transcendentalism that most differentiates it from the British Romantics—except for pre-Romantic Blake (1973, 167). He distills its functions to these three: as an idiom of

extended inventory and other synecdoches are, as much as
metaphor, based on deep analogy.

Actually, the inventory, while less important in the
rhetorics of, for example, Abraham Lincoln or the Native
Americans (Blaisdell 2000), is conspicuous and of great im-
portance in other rhetorics that inspired Thoreau, notably
Cicero, Milton (*Paradise Lost*), and Dante (*The Inferno*). It
also stands out in one of Thoreau's most basic, indeed sacred, texts: Homer, not only the obvious Catalogue of Ships
and the list-like sequences of warriors or mortal combats
around which entire books of the *Iliad* are structured, but
the extraordinary list of fourteen legendary and/or illustri-
ous women whom Odysseus meets in Hades. This is some
world literary context for the strikingly long lists in the
Gita and Thoreau.

The essential, articulated or expressed as part of the
whole, is matched, in the second place, by radical metaphors. "I am the seed," says Krishna (10.39), whereas in
Thoreau's poetics and rhetoric, alluding to one of his
master tropes, Captain John Brown is "an Angel of Light"
(in "A Plea for Captain John Brown" [2002, 279])—among
other extravagant equations. Great power is achieved when
such metaphors precede, bracket, or culminate a string of
synecdoches. "I am the creation and the dissolution of the
universe" (7.6) precedes the powerful image "On me all this
(universe) is strung, / Like heaps of pearls on a string" (7.7),
and then "I am taste in water" (7.8, Edgerton), followed by

---

democracy (all things are equal), an expression of exuberance, and its
workings as illustrative and symbolic (175). In fact, the list as key trope
was and is salient in undemocratic cultures, from that of Homeric Greece
to ancient Israel to Tsarist Russia. The inventory, far from being inherently and necessarily an expression of "exuberance," can be as tedious as
a laundry list. Finally, "illustrative and symbolic" are too vague to work as
defining terms. Buell does not mention the massive input regarding lists
from the East Indian classics, notably the Gita, which all of the Concord
Transcendentalists, unlike the British Romantics, were intensively reading
and extensively quoting from.

a long string of synecdoches. Comparably, Thoreau may cap a listing of a dozen or more plants by name (sometimes with the Latin in parentheses) with a particular sumac or "a perfect hemlock . . . standing like a pagoda" (135) that becomes a metaphor or simile of metamorphosis or faith in nature and Nature—or of beauty itself.

Both poets tend to eschew the all too familiar metaphors. What they do favor is a long sequence of lines, sentences, paragraphs, or stanzas of descriptive, meditative, or didactic text that involves little analogy. Then comes the abrupt transition to a climactic metaphor, that is, to a drastic analogy. For example, after nine stanzas on the indifference to opposites comes a great Gita list that Thoreau liked: "Whether seeing, hearing, touching, smelling, / Eating, walking, sleeping, breathing, / Talking, excreting, gasping, / Opening the eyes and shutting the eyes" (5.8–9, Edgerton), and then:

> Casting (all) actions upon Brahman,
>> Whose acts abandoning attachment,
> Evil does not cleave to him,
>> As water does not cleave to a lotus-leaf.
>> (5.10, Edgerton)

Such terminal tropes impart a torque to the poetics that resembles the lyric epiphany in epic texts (Friedrich 2000).

To take a second example, nine criteria for one who is "steady of insight" (*prajñana*) are wrapped up with this:

> And when he withdraws,
>> As a tortoise his limbs from all sides,
> His senses from the objects of sense,
>> His mentality is stabilized. (2.58, Edgerton)

Both of our authors share scores of tropes from the universal cross-cultural repertoire or reservoir of metaphors where, for example, thoughts are clouds and desire is fire. One of these is the culminating analogy that gets it together, or, in common parlance, the punch metaphor. Trivial or trite, some would aver, is the mere fact of the climactic metaphor, but its content and how it works in the present case are not.

Denial of Opposites (*dvandva-moha-nir-mukta*)

> This is the only way, we say; but there are as many ways as there can be drawn radii from one center. (*Walden*, 7)

The denial of opposites works in both poets in tandem with the affirmation of absolutes, and ramifies widely.

The opposites or antitheses denied in the Gita run to dozens, among which the following stand out: heat versus cold, good versus evil, light versus dark, and, deepest and most cited, joy or happiness versus pain or woe (4.22, 2.27, passim). Being subject to or acting out on the basis of these opposites is the fundamental form of illusion, and liberation from them is the sine qua non path to peace and the supreme good (see the following section, "Liberation from Delusion"). As put in the fifteenth book, using the translation by Wilkins, "... those who are free from contrary causes, whose consequences bring both pleasure and pain, are no longer confounded in their minds, and ascend to that place which endureth forever. Neither the sun, nor the moon, nor the fire enlighteneth that place from whence there is no return, and which is the supreme mansion of my abode" (15.5–6; see also 5.3, 7.28).[9] The Gita has one of its beautiful long compounds here which

---

9. The biblical tone of this and other passages from the Wilkins translation parallels the New Testament subtext discussed elsewhere.

Thoreau couldn't have known as such but to the sense
of which through translation he probably responded—
duality-delusion-negation-freed (*dvandva-moha-nir-mukta*), as
in the seventh book:

> But those in whom evil has come to an end,
> Those men whose actions are pure;
> They, *liberated from the deluding powers of the opposites,*
> Worship me with firm vows. (7.28)

Wilkins had a different take: "Those men of regular lives,
whose sins are done away, being freed from the fascination arising from contending passions, enjoy me" ([1785]
1959, 72).

The Gita may deny opposites while at other times en-
joining both of them: to take an example already stressed
earlier, one should strive toward supreme peace, on the
one hand, but, on the other hand, here on Kshetra Field
are seven reasons for killing your kin and so fight you
must. In form these opposites or false polarities run from
the linguistic[10] (many of the two-root compounds involve
opposites), to behavior or action (disciplined action versus
that driven by anger, fear, greed, or lust), to the purely
conceptual, ideational, or metaphysical—the demonic versus
the divine, "I am immortality and death; both being and
non-being" (9.19).

Thoreau does not inveigh against the illusion of opposites in the Gita style, but cunningly alludes to their
transcendence by inserting an aside that deconstructs its
immediate context; in the midst of a passage on the beauty
and purity of "The Ponds," we seem to hear a line of pure

---

10. While the word *dvandva*, meaning two-root compound, occurs only
four times (in three different derivations) in the Gita, *dvandva* compounds
occur scores of times, often as components of long (i.e., one-line) words
(of which I have counted 107 in the Gita).

Gita: "The thrills of joy and thrills of pain are indistinguishable" (127; parenthetically, one wonders what he actually meant here, "thrill" being one of his favorite words). Thoreau denies opposites by other ruses of his poetic practice, or by flouting standard, idiomatic associations: "I have a great deal of company in my house; especially in the morning, when nobody calls" (92); or by innovating within the phrase or by recoining a cliché, or by telling us the opposite of what we are conditioned to expect: for example, giving us the "society" in nature but a naturalist's perspective on the society of his villagers before their houses as a row of prairie dogs ("The Village"). These tactics and the strategy beneath them can generate oxymorons or seeming non sequiturs that have understandably irritated readers from his contemporaries to this day—what some call his fault of unlimited contradiction (Anderson 1968, 55).

Yet another Thoreauvian way of denying opposites is to stoutly affirm one in one place and the other, opposite one in a second: his daemonic and inspired dance at the foot of a rainbow is artfully counterbalanced by mischievous jigs with the devil elsewhere. In the very first sentence in "Higher Laws" he reports "a strange thrill of savage delight" on seeing a woodchuck and then being "strongly tempted to seize and devour him raw" (140), but in the middle of this same chapter we read, "Is it not a reproach that man is a carnivorous animal? . . . he will be regarded as a benefactor of his race who shall teach man to confine himself to a more innocent and wholesome diet . . . to leave off eating animals, as surely as the savage tribes have left off eating each other . . ." (144). His refusal to pay his poll tax and hence support war with Mexico (115) is balanced elsewhere by glib machismo about spitting a Mexican (108—implicitly with a bayonet, not roasting him as tenderloin as one scholar suggests—ironically, I hope [West 2000, 439]); earlier, the heroism of those who stood in the front lines at the bloody battle of Buena Vista in that same Mexican War is referred

to as a standard even while it is rhetorically belittled by an
invidious comparison with bravery in industry (e.g., the
"cheerful valor of the men who inhabit the snow-plough for
their winter quarters" [80]). In this Gita mood he can in one
place delight in, admire, and even relish war, or parody its
most brutal carnage, while at another enjoy tranquil meditation as a route to cosmic peace. On the political axis, his
essay "Resistance to Civil Government," which begins with
"That government is best which governs not at all," ends
with, "I will cheerfully obey those who know better and can
do better than I, and in many things even those who neither
know nor can do so well." Both statements are ironic, of
course. Thoreau's ironies regarding commerce and industry
have been well mined by Cavell (1981).

Let us conclude with additional, shared ways of denying
opposites. First, both poets achieve the goal by ingeniously
juxtaposing antonyms within the line or even the word: joy
and pain, raw meat versus a vegetarian diet, heroic warrior
versus antiwar activist, garrulous village gossip versus reclusive
hermit, the scimitar as cimeter or see-meter and, indeed,
the hundreds of puns and related etymological insights of
this punmaster in an age of consummate punsters (West
2000). Since illusion arises in part from the way the syntax
and vocabulary of any natural language encode polarities,
polarities should be linguistically challenged, played with,
bent and broken.

In the second place, opposites can be denied by jum-
bling the maximally abstract and the maximally concrete:
the maximally abstract idea of extension, for instance, is
illustrated in twenty Gita stanzas that range from the sun
to the Veda to horses and snakes to the beginning, the
middle, and the end of time (11.19–38). By way of contrast,
try to imagine the infinitely extended God of the cerebral
Spinoza—with a fat paunch and gory tusks—or any of the
lecherous coyotes of Native American lore pronouncing on
infinite extension, and yet this sort of synthesis marks both

our poets. Both poets, finally, move from despondency or despair or desperation in the midst of battle and similar struggles to the opposite pole of peace and harmony through identification with, as the case may be, Krishna or Nature. The way the two poets entertain opposites has been misinterpreted by the many critics who stay at the relatively superficial, verbal aspect of paradox, ambiguity, and exaggeration, to which, in Thoreau's case, we can add oxymoron, parody, and indirection (Golemba 1990, 205). To begin, astute study by Golemba and others (Matthiessen 1941, 166–75; Shanley 1957) of successive drafts of *Walden* and *A Week* has clearly shown that as Thoreau neared the end of his product he artfully increased indeterminacy, open-endedness, and seeming contradiction. At a deeper level, however, the Thoreau on opposites who affirms while he denies, synthesizes while he deconstructs, and the like, is motivated by the absolute principle of the denial of opposites, which, as already stressed here, are the root of illusion, hence of evil. The deeper thrust of *Walden*, governing the shallower levels, is toward a middle way that weaves between, integrates, collapses, or transcends opposites and dichotomies. Certain chapters, for example, make pairs—"Solitude" versus "Visitors" or "Higher Laws" versus "Brute Neighbors"—that Thoreau then deliberately transcends. The *Gita*, as has already been argued, is pervasively informed by the same strategy or, better, epistemology and ontology.

Let us once and for all list most of the Thoreauvian opposites that may be unified (Schneider 1975; Fischer 2003): nature versus culture, nature versus mind, rural versus urban, eternal versus transient, civilized East versus frontier West, Oriental East/the Ganges versus Euro-American West/the Concord River, good neighbor and fellow citizen versus defiant anarchist, traditional crafts versus the new technology, wildness versus personal cultivation, material versus spiritual, science versus poetry, physical versus mental, sensuous versus ascetic, concrete versus abstract, body

versus spirit, death versus (re)birth—and many others where
Thoreau splits the "versus" with the cimeter of his discern-
ment, seeing and representing himself (in "The Bean-Field"
chapter) as *both* Antaeus, whose strength was drawn from
the earth, and Hercules, who strangled and killed him by
holding him off the ground. In "Higher Laws" he defines
or at least describes the spiritual as the savage life but then
says that he reverences both (140). His case on the middle
way is made perhaps most brilliantly by the parable of the
sandbank that had been formed by a cut made for the
railroad, the steel monster of the new capitalist technology, but which when thawing revealed natural processes in
their complexity (while the railroad itself sounds, at times
and at a distance, like a partridge or a hawk). In typical
style, the indeterminacy of the middle way was increased
by Thoreau even while he also increased the authority of
Walden by references to the Bible, Islamic mystics, and many
other sacred or at least "great" texts.[11]

What were the main sources and inspirations for Thoreau's middle way? I have broached this in the first chapter,
but for now as follows. He certainly read and profited from
Samuel Taylor Coleridge and took extensive notes, yet his
middle way differs along all the main Coleridgean dimensions (that Emerson incorporated more naïvely): "the law
of opposites," "the reciprocal attraction of opposites," "the
unity of antitheses," and so forth (Barfield 1971). Coleridge
was *not* "the catalyst" (pace West 2000, 33; Johnson 1991;
et al.). Thoreau's middle way, on the contrary, owes much
more to the catalytic effect of earlier studies of Confucius
and Mencius: to pluck one example almost at random, "The

---

11. From another angle, however, Thoreau's theory (like some theories
of eros in Roman orthodoxy), posits a deep, primal wildness, some of
which evolves directly into the intellectual-spiritual-creative, while other
aspects evolve toward the "sensual," but can be turned or transmuted
into the spiritual.

Master said: 'When simplicity surpasses refinement, one is a rustic; when refinement surpasses simplicity, one is a scribe. Only when refinement and simplicity are well blended can one become a gentleman' " (*Analects* 6.18). And it owes yet more to his earlier study of the Gita with the many threads of Buddhism that are woven into it as critical components (e.g., Zaehner 1973, 215 passim; Upadhyaya 1971). The Concord Transcendentalists and their Boston-area critics, incidentally, saw the Gita as a mainly Buddhist text: as Lowell once asked mockingly: "Thor or Budh?" (1890, 362).[12] Thoreau's middle, Orient-derived way, precisely because it is usually hidden and hence at work insidiously, accounts in part for the continual global and—to date—timeless appeal of *Walden.*

Liberation from Delusion

Filled with hypocrisy, arrogance and pride,
Through delusion taking up false notions. (BG, 16.10)

Perhaps the master concept that unites the two poets and the scriptures that they authored is denoted, not by a single word, but by the compound concept of liberation from delusion that was introduced earlier.

Both poets start with the material world, the *Gita's prakṛti*, which includes not only objects such as a stone or one's hand, but psychological categories such as mind and egoism ("I-doer," or "I-maker") and cultural categories such as caste and above all the generic, all-cross-cutting opposites

---

12. While Thoreau scholars often see this as reflecting ignorance, it actually reflects a sound intuition of the partly Buddhist essence and origins of *Walden.* The exact nature of the Buddhist components in *Walden* calls for further research. Similarly, many striking passages in the Gita are part of a wider Buddhism: e.g., the turtle cited above features in the great white turtle poem by Chinese Buddhist Wang Wei.

or polarities that should be familiar to the reader by now.
The Gitaesque view corresponds roughly to Thoreau's: the
individual is immersed, indeed trapped, in a material and
materialistic world—the economic matter of a debasing and
exploitative political economy, the political matter of the
colonial, imperialistic and militarized government. Within
this Thoreauvian matter roil such evils as false patriotism
and hypocritical philanthropy. The material world is for
these poets both the content and the form of delusion.

Neither poet gives us a definition of delusion—
although Thoreau comes close, as in "Shams and delusions are esteemed for soundest truths" (65). Intimations
of the intensity of feeling involved for the Gita poet can
be had from the metaphors for delusion or the situation
within which a deluded person finds himself. The upside-
down tree, as we have seen, can be read as standing for
delusion. Otherwise: quagmire, turbid quicksands, thicket,
dense forest, net, snare, jungle and swamp of delusion.
These latter metaphors, all translations into English of a
multivocal symbol and its grammatical derivations, invalu-
ably reflect the intuitions of great scholars, translators, and
poets of the nuances of the Sanskrit root *moha-*, nuances that
Thoreau would have partially associated to when reading
Wilkins's suggestive translation. Thoreau in his puckish way
more than matches these glosses with extended and often
hilarious conceits where, for example, a man's furniture
and even the pieces of his dismantled shanty are dragged
like traps that will catch him and look for all the world like
"an enormous wen which had grown out of the nape of
his neck . . . If I have got to drag my trap, I will take care
that it be a light one and do not nip me in a vital part"
(45). Deluded men slave all their lives for "a questionable
liberty" (36). One of the most resonating, damning, and
oft-quoted claims in *Walden* is that "the mass of men lead
lives of quiet desperation" (5), that is, that the calm and

sure projects of most men are only a pretense or that they are deluding themselves both about the happy façade and the inner despair (Comey 2004). (Thoreau is explicit that the addressees of his critique are not only the men of Concord but of all his country. The Gita poet, while speaking primarily of excess, hypocrisy, power, and propriety in his kingdom, would seem to have all mankind in view.)

The idea of delusion, while not defined in the Gita, is enriched and clarified by dozens of associations and contexts, notably, on the negative side, with pride and power-tripping, indolence and sloth, and darkness and sleep: "Know dark inertia born of ignorance as the delusion of every embodied self; it binds one with negligence, indolence, and sleep, Arjuna" (14.8, Miller). More complex than these associations is the imbrication of delusion with hypocrisy, meaning roughly, to put on a false face regarding one's intentions when it comes to wealth, human relations, and religious ritual (see also chapter 5).

The meaning of delusion in the Gita stanzas on greed-driven hoarding, luxury, and wealth is more than matched by Thoreau's ideological pyrotechnics in "Economy" (see Cavell 1981, 88–89), with its mockery and excoriation of working for "excess" and—a favorite word—"trumpery" (45–46). For both poets the materialistic struggle for excess wealth, the most concrete form of delusion, is evil and sinful—emphatically for the Gita poet where, as with original sin in Christianity, you may fall into it at birth (7.27). Thoreau's hostility to greed and possessiveness and their consequences is perhaps distilled in his famous "Simplicity, simplicity, simplicity!" (62). "Shall we always study to obtain more of these things, and not sometimes to be content with less?" (24), he asks; or, "With respect to luxuries and comforts, the wisest have ever lived a more simple and meagre life than the poor . . . None can be an impartial or wise observer of human life but from the vantage ground of what *we* should call voluntary poverty" (9). Not only is materialistic struggle for wealth a sign of delusion, but wealth once acquired becomes a *source* of delusion.

The simple life, with or without ritual, is an escape from the toils and coils of delusion to a freedom from the material world that for the Gita poet includes the three "strands" of that world. For both poets the aspired-to liberation is, above all, from the opposites or what we would call the antimonies that are paradigmatic for all cultures, that is, that are cross-cultural universals (see "Denial of Opposites" earlier in this chapter). Liberation from dualities, making them nought (*nir-dvandva*), is for both poets to be achieved by various combinations of the three great disciplines of work, knowledge, and faith or devotion; the three disciplines are given different priorities at different times in different contexts so that it is better for the present purposes to list them as coordinate: as will be repeated later, Thoreau's "faith in a seed" (Thoreau 1993) is analogous to the Gita poet's faith in Krishna who is the seed of the universe (see "Faith" in chapter 8). Liberation from the material world and its entangling opposites leads to or is synergistic for both poets with a state of indifference, in which a piece of gold or a clod of earth are the same (6.8), or, in a famous stanza, "Learned men see with an equal eye a scholar and dignified priest, a cow, an elephant, a dog, and even an outcaste scavenger" (5.18, Miller), and, "Men who master the worldly world have equanimity" (5.19). The person who has achieved liberation (*moksha*) sees or knows the difference between two realms that are usually confused: matter, on the one hand, and primal spirit, on the other. These and other passages are paralleled by many in Thoreau where ostentatious and evil differences are leveled out, so that a man with many shanties is actually poorer than a man carrying one; human beings with their traits and foibles are reduced in an ontological egalitarianism (see "Denial of Opposites").

All these persuasive thoughts on delusion, the dualities, and the denial of difference imply a challenging agenda for the engaged sage, one that, if achieved, will carry beyond the sacred texts and the rituals they enjoin (2.57–71): "As the mountainous depths of the ocean are unmoved when waters rush into it, so the man unmoved when desires enter him attains a peace that eludes the man of many desires" (2.70, Miller). Thoreau similarly suggests a state of mind where, after reading timeless and beloved texts such as the *Iliad* and the Gita, one goes beyond them, freed from delusion. The last stage for both poets is the ascent from the sins of delusion to a higher state of being or consciousness marked by serenity, illumination, and insight.

This higher state of the Gita has two disparate meanings, however. One is total, the soul freed forever from the cycle of life. The second is relative, a higher state of mind achieved by some persons in some situations in the here-and-now while still not unentangled from the fateful round. Thoreau speaks of a state similar to this second one, more often than not in an exclusive sense, for "one in a million," couched in some of his finest sentences: "To him whose elastic and vigorous thought keeps pace with the sun, the day is a perpetual morning . . . To be awake is to be alive. I have never yet met a man who was quite awake. How could I have looked him in the face? . . . To affect the quality of the day, that is the highest of arts" (61). "If men would steadily observe realities only, and not allow themselves to be deluded, life, to compare it with such things as we know, would be like a fairy tale . . . we inhabitants of New England live this mean life that we do because our vision does not penetrate the surface of things. We think that that *is* which *appears* to be" (65). As the Gita puts it:

> When it is night for all creatures,
> a master of restraint is awake;
> when they are awake, it is night
> for the sage who sees reality. (2.69, Miller)

Both poets, then, extol the highest state of the few who are awake, versus the somnolence that fetters the great majority.

The fight against somnolence is first cousin to the fight against despondency with which the Gita begins and ends and which is but a concrete instance of the generic injunction, carried through many arguments, to liberate oneself from delusion. *Walden* starts with the author as a Chaucerian chanticleer crowing to wake his neighbors up and then, after a long and optimistic grappling with questions of despair, ends with a vision of the light of dawn that promises a new and ecstatic awareness. Both books are, then, orchestrated in terms of liberation from delusion.

There is a fuzzy but valid analogy between, on the one hand, the Gita poet coming to know his inner self and the higher reality of Krishna through action governed by duty and, on the other hand, Thoreau's realizing his inner, potential self and doing what he was called to do while reaching the god(dess) Nature through a life of simplicity, free of irrelevant attractions.

As a sort of coda to the aforementioned delineation of the many parallels between the Gita and *Walden* poets when it comes to their deeply shared value of liberation from delusion, it does remain to indicate certain critical differences. First, in the Gita lower-caste individuals are born deluded, and the state of being deluded is actually a product of the third strand of "dark inertia"; in other words, persons born darkly inert are *almost* irreparably deluded, and all persons with some of this dark inertia in their souls are subject to its baleful influences throughout their lives into subsequent lives. Thoreau, unlike the Gita poet, continuously makes liberation practical, achievable, local, and personal. More decisively, his main alternative to delusion is not, in the main, otherworldly existence, but an approximation to truth, be it the hard bottom of Reality or the hard fact that severs you when you perceive it (Bush 1985). The second Thoreauvian alternative is the fundamental value of Beauty, about which the Gita says nothing, and which one can approximate through fine-tuning one's senses—taking a walk at dawn! Finally, while the Gita poet strives to see clearly the abyss that yawns between the self (*ātman*) and the cosmos or oversoul, Thoreau's faith is not only in a seed but in the possibility that a person can reach a level of delicacy and intention where the boundaries between oneself and Nature become blurred and then dissolve, here and now.[13]

We may conclude with one of Thoreau's most complex and pregnant images of nature, reminiscent of the upside-down tree, the myriad colors of Walden Pond, and the ax/axis symbol: what one might refer to as the ice bubbles of delusion (and illusion?). These bubbles emerge as something "very clear and beautiful," but, following a trope of exact measurement and an account of the bubbles' various geometrical shapes, there are some subtle metamorphoses:

> The first ice is especially interesting and perfect, being hard, dark, and transparent . . . If you examine it closely the morning after it freezes, you find that the greater part of the bubbles, which at first appeared to be within it, are against its under surface, and that more are continually rising from the bottom; while the ice is as yet comparatively solid and dark, that is, you see the water through it. These bubbles are from an eightieth to an eighth of an inch in diameter, very clear and beautiful, and you see your face reflected in them through the ice. There may be thirty or forty of them to

---

13. The idea of liberation works as part of a complex family of nuances. "Liberation" and "liberty" (from *liber*, "free," and so forth) are associated with "deliberately" and its cogeners ("I went to the woods to live deliberately"), from *deliberare*, the latter from the word for scales, as in the zodiacal Libra. Both "free" and "to weigh," in turn, are connected by connotation with the Latin word for "inner bark," *liber*, that Thoreau was multilingually punning on.

a square inch. There are also already within the ice narrow oblong perpendicular bubbles about half an inch long, sharp cones with the apex upward; or oftener, if the ice is quite fresh, minute spherical bubbles one directly above another, like a string of beads . . . But as the last two days had been very warm, like an Indian summer, the ice was not now transparent, showing the dark green color of the water, and the bottom, but opaque and whitish or gray, and though twice as thick was hardly stronger than before, for the air bubbles had greatly expanded under this heat and run together, and lost their regularity; they were no longer one directly over another, but often like silvery coins poured from a bag, one overlapping another, or in thin flakes, as if occupying slight cleavages. The beauty of the ice was gone . . . (164–65)

Innumerable smaller bubbles form beneath the surface, and, Thoreau concludes, "the infinite number of minute bubbles which I had first seen against the under surface of the ice were now frozen in likewise, . . . each, in its degree, had operated like a burning glass on the ice beneath to melt and rot it" (165). Thoreau has given us a parable, rarely discussed since. True, it can be read as a metaphor of the seasons (which orchestrate *Walden*), or of the scientific process model to which he contributed, or of the endless Indic round of life, or as a totalizing symbol of the metamorphoses that hold us all in thrall, as represented in the Thoreau-favorite Ovid. But it is at least as likely that it is meant to be a parable of the delusions: from a measurable and "perfect" origin, the bubbles proliferate through time, interact, and end up, indeed, like "little air-guns" that "crack and whoop" (165) in the larger environment.

The Infinitudes, Especially of Time

I am infinite time. (BG, 10.33)

Time is but the stream I go a-fishing in. (*Walden*, 66)

Not till we have lost the world, do we begin to find ourselves, and realize where we are and the infinite extent of our relations. (*Walden*, 115)

One of the cornerstones on which both poets build their work is the fact of infinitude and the infinite ways that that fact can be suggested. In the Gita time (*kāla*) occurs only sixteen times, granted that many other stanzas involve or imply it. It is identified with Krishna in memorable stanzas: "I am infinite time" (10.33). It can be collapsed into a temporal One: the past, present, and future, the beginning, middle, and end of creation (10.32). It is cyclical: "in Brahma's cosmic realm worlds evolve in incessant cycles" (8.16, Miller)—a cyclicity of the concrete yet unimaginable day and night of Brahma (8.17–18), each *Kalpa* or temporal unit of day and night for one thousand times 4,340,000 years (Basham 1956, 320). At the dawning of one of these days all manifest things emerge from primal matter or the unmanifest, only to sink again at night into this same unmanifest infinitude (7.24). From another angle, Krishna is equated with the infinite extension of space within which all we creatures move like the wind (9.6), or, again, as already noted, he fills space in all directions (11.20). In the other direction, that of the infinitely microscopic, lies "the divine spirit . . . the primordial poet . . . smaller (more subtle) than an atom . . . unthinkable form, sun-colored beyond darkness" (8.9). In these grand vistas all categories collapse into a spacio-temporal black hole. If the cosmic upside-down tree stands for the "ontic terror" of chaos, as was previously suggested, it also stands for the infinitudes beyond chaos. These infinitudes that strike us as Pascalian are the ultimate, terminal, beyond-the-liminal reality of "the field."

Thoreau speaks to us of the infinitude of time with equally compelling words, be it of two eternities or of the infinite past and future collapsing into the present (11); his time, also cyclical, is conveyed, on the one hand, by what he writes about the four seasons and their recurrence; such time fits the concentric circles of Walden Pond and, indeed, some of the ideas, mathematical and otherwise, developed so brilliantly in Emerson's "Circles" essay. Thoreau's Gitaesque, cyclic time, on the other hand, interplays with the more familiar, Western, even Newtonian idea of time as linear, a line in the sand, a river or stream, the dawns of tomorrow, the infinities of the past and the future.

Let us go deeper into Thoreau's time. "Time" is the most frequent key word in *Walden*, occurring no less than 167 times or an average of almost once per page. The word is usually part of familiar idioms, such as Thoreau's favored "from time to time," which, while ostensibly "ordinary," are of great philosophical import because they may imply that time itself is an object that can be wasted, borrowed, and so forth (36, 37), as in "I lost my time into the bargain" (47). These idioms, moreover, illustrate what has been called "Standard Average European," with all its metaphysical implications (Whorf 1997, 152–59).[14] Other philosophical meanings are embedded in some of Thoreau's most memorable sentences, where time, for example, is not a Platonic absolute flowing apart from the events occurring

---

14. In a series of brilliant essays, Benjamin Lee Whorf (1997) developed this European idea of time as countable objects versus Native American models, notably Hopi, where time is a process of which the speaker is a part.

in it, but a stream in which Thoreau goes fishing (66), be it for pickerel or sincerity. In other key loci time is vaguely distinguished from eternity: "as if you could kill time without injuring eternity" (4). Thoreau sometimes mythologizes time and eternity, as in the following passage:

> I have occasional visits in the long winter evenings, when the snow falls fast and the wind howls in the wood, from an old settler and original proprietor, who is reported to have dug Walden Pond, and stoned it, and fringed it with pine woods; who tells me stories of old time and of new eternity; and between us we manage to pass a cheerful evening with social mirth and pleasant views of things, even without apples or cider . . . An elderly dame, too, dwells in my neighborhood, invisible to most persons, in whose odorous herb garden I love to stroll sometimes, gathering simples and listening to her fables; for she has a genius of unequalled fertility, and her memory runs back farther than mythology, and she can tell me the original of every fable, and on what fact every one is founded, for the incidents occurred when she was young. A ruddy and lusty old dame, who delights in all weathers and seasons, and is likely to outlive all her children yet. (93)

At several points he contrasts empirical or grammatical time with a transcendent temporal reality that of course lies beyond definition or description, as in, "That time which we really improve, or which is improvable, is neither past, present, nor future" (67; see also p. 75). This idea of a collapsed time is not congruent with any Standard Average European, but it does resemble the Gita's Krishna: "I am time, the cause of world destruction" (11.32); "Of creations,

I am the beginning and the end, and also the middle"
(10.32). Krishna is not only all times but a time beyond
time, as in Thoreau's real time.

The infinitude of eternity in Thoreau, as in the Gita,
is analogous to the infinitude of space: "This whole earth
which we inhabit is but a point in space" (90), and, "It would
be easy to cut their threads any time with a little sharper
blast from the north. We go on dating from Cold Fridays
and Great Snows; but a little colder Friday, or greater snow,
would put a period to man's existence on the globe" (169).
He makes time and space concrete through images of the
endless sky or man's idea that there can be lakes without bottoms. For both poets, then, time and space are unbounded,
be it in the collapse of the past, present, and future, or the
ungraspable extent of the images of Krishna.

These have critical associations. First of all, temporal
and spatial infinitude is linked in the Gita to perfection.
Thoreau, going further, links Hindu *Kalpa* not just to infinite perfection but to its achievement. His fabled artist of
Kouroo "made no compromise with Time, Time kept out of
his way, and only sighed at a distance because he could not
overcome him" (218), until the wonderful staff was finished.
In Thoreau this transcendence of time through perfection,
incidentally, is congruent with a belief in universals: "The
oldest Egyptian or Hindoo philosopher raised a corner of
the veil from the statue of the divinity; and still the trem-
bling robe remains raised, and I gaze upon as fresh a glory
as he did, since it was I in him that was then so bold, and
it is he in me that now reviews the vision" (67). Universals
transcend time.

Second of all, both poets locate infinitude most urgently
in the hour or instant of death. Six stanzas in the Gita speak
of the "end-time" of death. The word itself for time, *kāla*,
implies death and is so translated at times; it is not synony-
mous but overlaps with death in other Indian texts. The
universal fact of death and the "hour" of it are a totalizing

experience when man, freed from illusion and with faith, can "know" Krishna in all his infinities. As for Henry Thoreau, recall the ever-present possibility of death, be it in terms of the chill creeping up one's legs and the death rattle in one's throat (66), or, as noted earlier, the earthly speck on which we, circling through space, could perish at any moment and the death in January 1842 of *both* Henry's beloved older brother John and Ralph Waldo Emerson's darling son "little Waldo" (Richardson 1995, 358). The awareness of death is linked with a consciousness of infinitude.

Let us make a formalist excursus to the connection between Thoreau's ideas of infinity and the actual, partly iconic form of the sentences in which these ideas are couched. In Thoreau the infinitudes are suggested by a syntax where the sentence is not a potentially infinite set resulting from the application of recursive rules, but a meander that, the reader sometimes feels, originated back there somewhere and might go on forever. *Walden* has many more than centipedal sentences, especially in the first chapter, where ten run to over two hundred words in length, and one to over three hundred (Davis 2002). Unlike the equally monstrous sentences of his soulmate and near age-mate, Leo Tolstoy (1828–1910), the constituents of Thoreau's sentences are not ordered into a Ciceronian syntactic pyramid of superordinate and subordinate phrases and clauses. Thoreau's long sentences, on the contrary, realize his etymology of wandering (*vagare*) extra far in an "extravagant way" ("I fear chiefly lest my expression may not be *extravagant* enough, may not wander far enough beyond the narrow limits of my daily experience" [216]), and so become themselves a metaphor for his philosophy. His endless sentences, like his extended inventories, may be tightly closed off—the lily that completes the ten riverine flowers—but many are not.

The most striking thing about time in Thoreau, to conclude, is his radical philosophy of the here-and-now, which for many readers resonates with modern phenomenology or existentialism. Words on the ultimate reality of the *now* run throughout *Walden*: for example, "God himself culminates in the present moment" (75), "the meeting of two eternities, the past and the future, which is precisely the present moment" (11).

Thoreau on time is neither Platonic, Aristotelian, nor Kantian, then, although there is some input from these philosophers, mainly through the Latin and English poetry that were second nature to him. Thoreau's phenomenology of the ultimate *now* seems, rather, to owe much to the idea of the moment of truth, of full realization, of "a drenching of reality" (66), ideas that are spread through the Gita and the allied Buddhist texts that were input to it. "This is the place of the infinite spirit; achieving it, one is freed from delusion; abiding in it [i.e., the infinite spirit] even at the time of death, one finds the calm of pure infinity" (2.72, Miller).

Thoreau goes beyond the Gita, however, in his vision of how unimaginable stretches of time can collapse into one blinding moment of total beauty. Let us return to the artist of Kouroo, who, his perfect work achieved, sees that "the former lapse of time had been an illusion, and that no more time had elapsed than is required for a single scintillation from the brain of Brahma to fall on and inflame the tinder of a mortal brain" (218)—alluding, once again, to the master symbol of light. Thoreau's thoughts on time give an intimation of what lies beyond the powers of language, which, of course, are never adequate (Friedrich 2009). The Kouroo parable is a good example, moreover, of how Thoreau sees (the achievement of) beauty as a redemption from time and, beyond that, eternity.[15]

---

15. Thoreau's notions of time and eternity become clearer if we relate two statements with great specific gravity: how can we "kill time [e.g., fritter it away meaninglessly] without injuring eternity" (4), which is condensed into "the present moment" (11, 75).

Chapter Eight

Three Ways to God

My basic concerns are not with genre, but both texts are called scriptures—one always has been, the other ever since Shanley's judicious classification (1957). Both propound three ways to a reality that we can call "God" (as opposed to the unequivocal God) for reasons to be given anon. In both, the three ways are at one level coordinate, feeding into each other, but at another level they are hierarchized, from the lowest kind, work, to the ultimate path of faith. Both advocate early on—the Gita in songs three through six, *Walden* in the first and second chapters—various kinds of work or action, such as raising beans, or study, as means to approach the divine and one's own salvation. Both, as noted, advocate that one act in accordance with duty, unattached, undistracted by the (possible) fruits of action. The Gita enjoins this dozens of times. Thoreau writes, "The true husbandman will cease from anxiety, as the squirrels manifest no concern whether the woods will bear chestnuts this year or not, and finish his labor with every day, relinquishing all claim to the product of his fields, and sacrificing in his mind not only his first fruits but his last fruits also" (112).

In the second place, both authors engage with many epistemological issues, since knowledge not only contributes to action and benefits from it but is also a means of escape from the material round and a way of entering into the divine and timeless; work and knowledge overlap in many ways. Thirdly, both books, the Gita scripture and the

117

Walden quasi-scripture, especially as one approaches their final, eighteenth units, urge the listener to faith, devotion, and love of God as the most powerful means to redemption and the saving of one's soul. While it is easy and indeed tempting to exaggerate the commonalities, obscured as they are by differences of cultural paradigm, idiom and vocabulary, and situation, the three ways, generically defined, work both as absolutes in their own right and as means or avenues to the two ideas of final cause or reality: Krishna or Nature—that is, God.

Preamble: *Yoga*

To some extent, and at rare intervals, even I am a yogi. (H. D. Thoreau, in a letter to H. G. O. Blake, 1849)

The word *yoga* (from *yuj*, the Sanskrit root for *yoke*), and the many compounds in which it figures, occurs over 150 times, almost ubiquitously, throughout the Gita. Yoga is the main subject of entire books, notably two through six: spiritual yoga (2), yoga of action or work (3), yoga of knowledge (4), yoga of renunciation (5), and the man of yoga (6), or, in Zaehner's delightful gloss, the athlete of the spirit. The control and self-discipline of *yoga* may be a means to purity and serenity, as in 6.45: "Then this vigorously striving yogin goes on the ultimate journey, cleansed of evil and perfected in numerous lives." Yoga in such larger scope means a physically, emotionally, and cognitively integrated way of life that will lead to liberation from dualities, and to a sense for the sameness of all things and to indifference to the fruits of action.[1] "As a candle flame stationed in a wind-

---

1. Yoga unbinds the bonds of suffering—for which there is a beautiful one-word line: *duhkha-saṁ-yoga-vi-yoga*.

less place does not flicker—runs the traditional simile—so is a yogin, restrained in thought and a practitioner of self-discipline" (6.19) or, in Edgerton's translation:

> As a lamp stationed in a windless place
> Flickers not, this image is recorded
> Of the disciplined man controlled in thought,
> Practicing discipline of the self.

Yoga practice creates a consciousness that will yoke one to the divine purposes of Krishna, the lord of yoga, in the three fundamental ways: of action, knowledge and insight, and faith and devotion. Gita yoga, as noted, opposes extreme asceticism. Glosses of *yoga*, incidentally, as discipline, steadfastness, integration of the spirit and steadfastness of the spirit, catch various aspects of the untranslatable.

Some of Thoreau's yoga, notably the value of simplicity, owes much to the Bible, the Latin Stoics, and the Puritan tradition that he inherited and adapted—simplicity in the face of a wasteful, luxury-oriented and destructive political economy—but this reinforces rather than mitigates the massive input from the Gita and the Laws of Manu. The goal of all these yoga practices and positions, as for the Gita, was to gain freedom from the destructive prisons of illusion, false ideology, and the mendacious paradigms of life. On the one hand, Thoreau's yoga, like the Gita's, is from page two on qualified by an attack on self-inflicted, tortuous penance:

> What I have heard of Bramins sitting exposed to four fires and looking in the face of the sun; or hanging suspended, with their heads downward, over flames; or looking at the heavens over their shoulders "until it becomes impossible for them to resume their natural position, while from the twist of the neck nothing but liquids can pass into

the stomach"; or dwelling, chained for life, at the foot of a tree; or measuring with their bodies, like caterpillars, the breadth of vast empires; or standing on one leg on the tops of pillars—even these forms of conscious penance are hardly more incredible and astonishing than the scenes which I daily witness. (2)

His yoga, like the Gita's, includes a wide range of positive activities and practices, ritualized, semi-ritualized, or not ritual at all: observation of nature, study of the great texts, writing, and ecstatic realization: "To some extent, and at rare intervals, even I am a yogi."

The marked if circumscribed differences between the Gita and *Walden* when it comes to sense perception and sensuousness are, as suggested before, dominated by deeper affinities. Most basic in the Gita is its ideology of the three "strands" of material nature that are mentioned off and on throughout and constitute the main burden of chapters fourteen, seventeen, and, in particular, the final movement of this song (which is orchestrated so well it is a verbal symphony). The highest or *sattvik* strand is defined with the yoga values of relinquishment, renunciation, lucidity, freedom from attachment, purity, constancy of mind, tranquility, light, self-control, patience, and honesty: "Observing solitude, barely eating, restraining speech, body, and mind; practicing discipline in meditation, cultivating dispassion" (18.52, Miller). Such values pervade *Walden* and the *Journal* and deeply influenced Thoreau, as did the absolute value of faith or *bhakti*.

Despite these similarities, the two poets differ in other ways. On the one hand, the theory and practice of yoga for the Gita poet is to control, constrain, and even curb the responses of the senses to the objects of sense, as in the simile cited earlier:

And when he withdraws,
    As a tortoise his limbs from all sides,
His senses from the objects of sense,
    His mentality is stabilized. (2.58, Edgerton)

Thoreau controls the senses for two reasons: first, Gita-like, to make them independent from what he calls the sensual, reptilian, animal, while admitting that this is ultimately impossible since these things are part of us. At another, anti-Gita level, Thoreau, aspiring to a life that is pure but also sensuous (147), seeks to cultivate and attune the senses for the fullest possible appreciation of sense objects—from the aroma of huckleberries to the flight of a hawk. As Thoreau puts it, "And we are enabled to apprehend at all what is sublime and noble only by the perpetual instilling and drenching of the reality that surrounds us" (122). In these senses, few writers in world literature, including such obvious candidates as his near contemporary Charles Baudelaire, have been as sensuous in their appreciation of sense objects and in the language they use to express and convey that appreciation—an invidious comparison that is if anything sharpened by the fact that Thoreau's sensuous appreciation did not include the delights (and torments) of lust.

Work (*karma*)

Most concretely, work in the Gita means a range of ritual practices that are referred to in many places: "Let him set up for himself a firm stool in a pure spot, neither too high nor too low, with a cover of cloth, deerskin, or Kusa grass" (6.11, van Buitenen). Work, as noted, is the theme of the third song, and is mentioned elsewhere at many points, typically referring to strenuous effort or action in anticipation of it such as girding oneself for battle (van Buitenen

1998, 17). Work encompasses all the daily round in peace or war, of men and women of all social classes.

Thoreau's point of view of work corresponds with the Gita's at all levels, starting with meditation in a sitting position, and clean habits for the temple of the body, including its diet: "There is something essentially unclean about this diet and all flesh . . . The practical objection to animal food in my case was its uncleanness . . . The repugnance to animal food is not the effect of experience, but is an instinct" (143). Like the Gita poet, Thoreau names optimal locations: the doorstep, the foot of a pine tree, the middle of Walden Pond. Also like the Gita poet, Thoreau enjoins discipline of the self, physical and mental, and was indeed a disciplined writer, reader, and "heroic reader"; in some years his work in terms of journal pages, pages of books written and rewritten, essays, and reading and study was extraordinary (Richardson 1986, 195 passim).[2] Thoreau's life and writing are consistent with all the features of yoga cited here and yet others: the pure and simple life, including chastity, the goal of serenity and peace of mind—here and in the afterlife.

Knowledge

> . . . it carries away one's understanding
> As the wind carries away a ship on the waters.
>   (2.67, Sargeant)

Knowledge and the quest for it are, with their associations, basic values for both poets. By the same token, both will be

---

2. By "heroic reader," here and elsewhere, Thoreau meant something like our "close reader": slow, repeated reading, attention to etymologies and subtext, "entering into" the text as an act of the imagination, and so forth.

discussed synthetically here rather than seriatim. Many of my points about knowledge tie back to earlier segments of this study and hence do not call for supportive citations.

The Gita poet seeks knowledge through solitary meditation, and the stated purpose of the *Walden* project was to live "deliberately," that is, thoughtfully, cognitively, getting to the bottom of meanings. The field of knowledge that the Gita field-worker tries to command, work in, and learn from is paralleled by what Thoreau says about his bean-field in the chapter with that name: he hoes navy beans but hopes to raise spiritual and ethical ones someday. Both poets repeatedly praise the knower or seer and neither ever criticizes or mocks a person in this exalted status—which both occupy at least at times and see themselves as occupying. For both the acquisition of knowledge is through discipline, or yoga, and for both the practice and mastery of such discipline entails a synthesis of qualified physical and mental asceticism leading to ecstatic vision. For both the idea and the ideal of knowledge is subdivided in terms of at least two further subdivisions: the first is of higher knowledge or "discrimination" versus lower rational, systematic, logic-oriented knowledge; the second is of empirical knowledge derived from experience versus transcendental knowledge, be it of time and space, or God and Nature. For both poets knowledge is part of a large set of positive values, notably purity, lucidity, chastity, and the simple life. For both the light of knowledge and knowing are radically contrasted with ignorance, be it the dark "sin" of ignorance in the Gita, which is interwoven—sometimes identified with—the sin of delusion, or be it, in *Walden*, the ignorance shared by most citizens of Concord and indeed the majority of mankind of the great books and their attendant spiritual values, as well as ignorance generically speaking. Knowledge and the possession of it, in other words, are for both poets diagnostic features of an intellectual elite: the virtuous Brahmin and others who in some sense know the Vedas or whose knowledge transcends it; the tiny fraction of Thoreau's friends and "the one in a million" who read great books or are "awake" in a larger sense. For both poets, the idea and the ideal of knowledge generate more metaphoric expressions than anything else: consider the boat, fire and other kinds of light, the sword or scimitar of knowledge that severs the roots of the upside-down tree, and other epistemic symbolism. Early on in the Gita, in book two (67), we hear that "if a mind (faculty of perception) is guided by the roving senses, it steals one's true wisdom (insight, understanding) as a wind a ship at sea," or as Wilkins translated it, "The heart, which followed the dictates of the moving passions, carried away his reason, as a wind the bark in a raging storm." Two songs later we hear, as was cited previously, "Even if you are the worst criminal of them all, you will cross over all that's crooked (evil, villainous), the tortuous stream of life on the (life) boat of transcendent knowledge" (4.36). Paralleling these images, Thoreau in the eighth chapter "launches himself" from "The Village," and then carries us through a dozen nautical or sea sailing related terms (tempestuous, set sail, snug harbor, merry crew, outer man at the helm, weather, storms, and so forth) without ever identifying himself or his mind as a ship. The two poets, in sum, are linked by their analogous figuration of knowledge.[3]

The poets have similar views on the intimate relation between knowledge and action. On the one hand, for both, knowledge outranks action; as the Gita words it, "As natural fire, O Arjuna, reduceth wood to ashes, so may the fire of wisdom reduce knowledge to ash" (4.37). On the other hand, action itself leads to knowledge even while it is an output of knowledge, and action rivals knowledge as a means to salvation. Both poets are concerned with bridging between knowledge and action, or, as Thoreau puts

---

3. The Thoreauvian pilot is part of, in concord with, the sea, like the tiny fisherman in a Chinese scroll painting—and not opposed to it by *principio individuationis*, à la Schopenhauer and, following him, Richardson.

it, between the philosopher and "the hero" (*Journal*, April 1840). One of the crowning achievements of the Gita was to connect knowledge and action by its injunction to act out of duty while not getting entangled in desire and the results of action. Thoreau was not convinced by the Gita's argument and he did not, in *Walden*, achieve or even set himself the goal of achieving a compromise, but when we take that main work together with his political essays such as "Civil Disobedience" and "A Plea for Captain John Brown," and his own personal political activism, we find that he did achieve such a compromise (see chapter 9).

Both poets, finally, vividly depict the problem of being lost, be it in the illusion of polarities or the mendacious ideologies of the day, after which some may find themselves. In Thoreau: "Every man has to learn the points of the compass again as often as he awakes, whether from sleep or any abstraction. Not until we are lost, in other words, not till we have lost the world, do we begin to find ourselves, and realize where we are and the infinite extension of our relations" (115). Being lost is further illuminated by the Gita: the man of restraint, endowed with wisdom, walks "in the night of time . . . when all things rest" (2.69), whereas Thoreau, in the aforementioned nautical passage, finds his way home from Concord through the woods in the night, the dark of night ("night," "dark," or both together occur seven times in one page). The meaning of the metaphor of being lost at sea or in the night and then finding one-self has been drawn out and deepened by Thoreau and then marvelously opened up and made problematical and suggestive: it is not knowledge that gets us across the sea of ignorance; rather, only by first losing ourselves and our ship of inadequate knowledge can we find ourselves again and ways to better understanding.[4]

---

4. A possible oblique co-source for the above in Thoreau is Matthew 10.39 (or 16.25): "He that findeth his life shall lose it, and he that loseth his life for my sake shall find it."

Faith (*śraddhā*)/Loving Devotion (*bhakti*)

> Though I do not believe that a plant will spring
> up where no seed has been, I have great faith
> in a seed. Show me that you have a seed there,
> and I am prepared to expect wonders. (Thoreau
> 1993, vi)

Śraddhā

Faith (*śraddhā*) in the sense of unqualified belief and a
total giving of the self to God in some sense is partly the
content of both works and reflexively guides their persuasive
arguments. In both works faith is distilled and symbolized
in ritual acts. As the Gita puts it in 13.10: "a constant and
invariable worship paid to me alone; worshipping in a private
place, and a dislike of the society of men" (Wilkins [1785]
1959, 102)—which rings like a page from *Walden*, where
faith is also realized in a wide variety of ritual(ized) acts:
"Every morning was a cheerful invitation to make my life
of equal simplicity, and I may say innocence, with Nature
herself. I have been as sincere a worshipper of Aurora as
the Greeks. I got up early and bathed in the pond; that
was a religious exercise, and one of the best things which
I did" (60). Thoreau's rituals of faith included not just
auroral skinny dips but the identification of botanical spe-
cies, long walks—usually meanderings in form—and, above
all, the reading of classics, and writing, and hoeing beans.
Beans become analogous to "sincerity, truth, simplicity, faith,
innocence, and the like" (110), the seed of which he also
aspires to cultivate.

Both poets sharply contrast acting in and for faith with
acting under false pretenses, hypocritically (see "Sincerity/
Hypocrisy" in chapter 5). Both excoriate the faithless majority: "How vigilant we are! Determined not to live by faith if
we can avoid it!" (7). As the Gita puts it in 17.3:

A man is made of faith,
Whatever faith he has, thus he is. (Sargeant)

For Thoreau faith is to a vision of God's face in a rainbow as the architect's shelf of bricks is to the arch that he will spring when he is building a cathedral (Boudreau 1990, 100).

Both poets have a concept of a deep faith that is deeper than any specific ritual or religion, a concept that even goes beyond (the study of) the Vedas or the "heroic reading" of great books. This shared idea of deep faith (17.17) also means that any and all religious forms can reach Krishna:

> I grant unwavering faith
> to any devoted man who wants
> to worship any form
> with faith. (7.21, Miller)

And later,

> When devoted men sacrifice
> to other deities with faith
> they sacrifice to me, Arjuna,
> however aberrant the rites. (9.23, Miller)

This deep faith of both poets is linked to the other two functional absolutes of knowledge and good action because all are means to "fair worlds" (18.70–72). For both poets the idea of faith is linked semiotically to the fundamental and never parodied absolute of simplicity—the simple, virtuous life without excess or arrogance. For both, faith cannot be realized without discipline/yoga, and in some degree discipline *is* faith and true faith *is* a discipline: faith without discipline is like clouds split apart (6.37–38). For both poets faith is a great liberating force that can free one from evil, delusion, and the daily grind:

Men who constantly practice
This teaching of Mine,
Believing, not sneering
Are also released from the bondage of action.
    (3.31, Sargeant)

While the relative power or priority of the disciplines has
generated much valuable commentary, it seems likely from
the overall orchestration, even teleology, of the Gita that faith
and devotion (*bhakti*), featured in the eighteenth and last
book, are the most powerful means to "the supreme way."
Thoreau, after almost eighteen chapters that call on those
who are desperate or of little faith, comes home on the final two pages with the parable of the "strong and beautiful
bug," who, after sixty years in the leaf of a kitchen table,
and more still in the living tree from which it was made,
gnawed its way out to emerge before "the astonished family
of man, as they sat around the festive board": "Who does not
feel his faith in a resurrection and immortality strengthened
by hearing of this?" (222–23).[5] From the chanticleer in the
first sentence to this miraculous insect in the next to last
paragraph, *Walden* is a call to faith.

    Thoreau's idea of faith is couched initially in terms of
the Vedas: "I am far from regarding myself as one of those
privileged ones to whom the Ved refers when it says, that 'he
who has true faith in the Omnipresent Supreme Being may
eat all that exists . . . [in] the time of distress' " (145–46).
But his real meaning emerges much more profoundly in
the whole page devoted to his close friend, Amos Bronson
Alcott (1799–1888), "One of the last of the philosophers . . . I
think that he must be the man of the most faith of any
alive . . . A true friend of man; almost the only friend of hu-

5. (Similar feelings of faith were inspired in many by the apparent dis-
covery in 2005 [since disproved—it was probably a Northern Pileated
Woodpecker] of the "extinct" ivory-billed woodpecker in the bottomland
swamp forest of eastern Arkansas.)

man progress . . . with unwearied patience and faith making plain the image engraven in men's bodies . . . A blue-robed man, whose fittest roof is the overarching sky which reflects his serenity. I do not see how he can ever die; Nature cannot spare him" (179–80).

The cardinal value of faith arouses an ancient debate when juxtaposed with the equally valued and axiomatic goal of avoiding delusion, particularly that entailed by opposites. Does not the idea of faith, on the one hand, imply that we leave unquestioned the ultimate sources of delusion? And does not the commitment to liberation from delusion, on the other, mean that nothing can be accepted unquestioningly? This seeming paradox, like that of the fruit of the tree of knowledge, does not bear on the complex argument of the two books in question, because of their fundamental assumption of absolutes (see chapter 3). These absolutes may be negative—dark ignorance, or hypocrisy and cowardice in action—or they may be positive, notably sincerity and purity. There may be irony, as with purity, as we have seen, or qualifications, as with sacrifice, but the values themselves are as absolute and unquestioned as Nature or Krishna. It is faith in this context of a dualistic value system that contributes to the deep moral code of both texts and that has contributed to their status and function as scripture—especially among "lay" readers who are not specialists. By a contradiction that both poets tolerate, the denial of opposites need not be predicated on the reality of the opposition between opposite and non-opposite.

Bhakti

The concept of faith in the two poets, and Thoreau in particular, leads us directly into the related and indeed overlapping concept of *bhakti*; *bhakti* is "the most cardinal doctrine in the *Gita*" (Edgerton 1952, 70), more so than the denial of opposites and others that have been discussed here. The concept of *bhakti* is predicated, first of all, on that of the individual spirit or soul that is capable of being indifferent to the things of this world and is not attached to the fruits of work—a stance that Thoreau advocates in *Walden*. *Bhakti*, second, is predicated on the possibility of a personal god who may take the form of Krishna as the charioteer, or Walden Pond, or be manifested in a lotus or a lily or the howl of a loon. Beyond, beneath, or above these manifestations is the abstract, imperishable, and eternal divine, difficult to grasp and understand, and in fact reached by only a few. But "grasp" is the wrong metaphor because the relation or bond between the individual self and the supernatural is one of reciprocated love, a sharing of what is held in common (*bhaj-*, "share"). The spiritual self, moreover, is yoked (*yuj-*), not like a team of horses pulling a chariot, but rather like halves of a twosome coupled together. There is a "mutual in-dwelling" (Carman 1987) between the two that are yoked. These feelings and emotions of devotion-and-love—and they are that and not ideas ordered by logic—are the main avenue and means to the crucial goal of liberation from delusion (and illusion), to the light of salvation from "the ocean of death and rebirth" (12.7; literally, Sargeant's "death-transmigration-ocean," *mṛtyu-saṁsāra-sāgarat*). The three paths to God are interrelated, as Upadhyaya has put it with great precision: action leads to *bhakti* (18.49–54), action leads to knowledge (4.38, 18.36–50), *bhakti* leads to action (10.10), *bhakti* leads to knowledge (10.11, 11.54), knowledge leads to action (10.7), and to *bhakti* (11.13 passim). A similar round-robin could be constructed for knowledge, action, and faith in Thoreau. But of the three, *bhakti* is probably the most powerful and basic, reminiscent in some ways of St. Paul.[6] Whether the

---

6. The many striking parallels and connections between the teachings of the apostle Paul and the Gita have been dealt with *en passant* by Zaehner (1973) but call for fuller articulation. Since the Gita was most probably composed about 200 BC, the borrowing, if there was any, must have been from East to West.

supernatural or god is beneficent or loving is actually left open at points in the Gita, just as in the writings of Thoreau. Perhaps the best overall definition of *bhakti* is this: loving, reciprocal devotion between the supernatural powers that be and the individual self—from the latter's point of view (Carman 1987).

And what is the relation between *bhakti* and faith? In the Gita, as already indicated, faith is a subset, a separately defined part of *bhakti*. In Thoreau faith is well defined through many uses, whereas the concept of *bhakti* is implied polysemously by faith, love, and other charged words and symbols. Thoreau never mentions *bhakti* (the Wilkins translation that he used does not give the Sanskrit in transliteration), but the generic idea, what I would call the "spirit of *bhakti*," informs *Walden* throughout and actually cries out toward the end. The *bhakti* torque of *Walden*'s last, eighteenth chapter matches in spirit the cumulative rise toward *bhakti* in the climactic statements of the eighteenth song of the Gita.

Chapter Nine

The Gita within *Walden*
Expanded: A Poetics
for Activism

Walden is among other things a tract of political education, education for membership in the polis. It locates authority in the citizens and it identifies citizens—those with whom one is in membership—as "neighbors."

—Stanley Cavell, *The Senses of Walden*

As a preamble to what follows, I find I want to wrap up the foregoing with some needed clarifications. I find it irritating that the Gita is stereotyped by many as a charter for asceticism (often seen as a perversion), the Indian caste system (which by any other name would smell as foul), and other negative things. And I have been outraged repeatedly by the way many persons stereotype Thoreau as a lifelong recluse who lived in a hut hermit-style and, as one colleague of mine phrased it, was "self-serving and asocial."

Thoreau lived on Walden Pond for two years as an "experiment," a model followed by many of his contemporaries: he walked into Concord several times a week to gossip, visit, eat his mother's pies, and hear the news. He acted socially and politically as a writer, lecturer, and citizen in Concord and indeed New England all his life. Today he stands as fundamental and formative in the defense of civil liberties, in the cause of environmentalism, in opposition to war, be it colonial or reflecting governmental militarism, and in condemning human exploitation of all kinds (not of only slaves but, for example, indebted farmers anywhere), and he stands as a champion of the higher law of individual conscience in the face of state tyranny—an awesome catalogue for someone who was primarily a naturalist, pencil-maker, and lyrical prosaist. He seems relevant now, even prescient.

It would be hard and unrealistic at this point to disentangle physical activism from activist writing, so let us consider them together in chronological order to see how the Gita of India pans out as Concord practice.

1. In 1844, when Emerson was to give a speech on the emancipation in the West Indies, the town selectmen not giving permission to have the bell rung, Thoreau went and rang it.

2. From 1845 to 1847, while he was sojourning on Walden Pond, "slaves were sometimes brought to him there but obviously there was no possible concealment in his house . . . so he would look after them by day, and by nightfall get them to his mother's or some other house of hiding," as reported by Emerson's son, Edward (Gougeon 1990, 152).

3. During the 1840s and 1850s, Thoreau's writings were punctuated by political agendas. The *Walden* chapter called "The Village" describes his being seized and jailed for a night because he did not want to recognize the authority of "the state which buys and sells men, women, and children, like cattle at the door of its senate-house" (115). In "Baker Farm" he writes that "the only true America is . . . where the state does not endeavor to compel you to sustain . . .

slavery and war and other superfluous expenses" (138). In these passages as elsewhere in his writings Thoreau connects the fight against slavery with resistance to imperialism and war.

4. Throughout the 1840s and 1850s, likewise, the Thoreau home (shared by his parents and two sisters) was "a nest of Abolitionists," a station in the Underground Railroad; "Rarely a week went by without some fugitive being harbored overnight in town and sped along his way before daylight. Henry Thoreau more than any other man in Concord looked after them, she said, caring for them for the night, purchasing their tickets, escorting them to the station— . . . —or for further protection accompanying them on the train for a while" (Harding 1965, 346–50; as reported by Mrs. Edwin Bigelow, "the acknowledged leader of Concord's participants in the Underground Railroad.")[1]

5. In 1848, "Resistance to Civil Government" was published for the first time. It advocated the idea that individual conscience, part of the rights of the individual, was higher than any civil law; if the machine of government "requires you to be the agent of injustice to another, then, I say, break the law. Let your life be a counter friction to stop the machine" (Rossi 1992, 233). Throughout "Resistance," Thoreau, again, linked antislavery with anti-imperialism: new slave states such as Texas would result from the Mexican War. "Resistance" and related speeches were delivered in many Massachusetts venues in the 1850s while civil war was raging in "Bleeding Kansas."

---

1. Three hundred and thirty-two slaves were eventually returned under the Fugitive Slave Law, of which eleven were eventually freed (Gougeon 1990, 152).

6. On July 4, 1850, Thoreau lashed out with his fiery "Slavery in Massachusetts" at a meeting of radical abolitionists in Worcester that was protesting the Compromise of 1850 with its Fugitive Slave Act, which soon resulted in the return in manacles of runaway slaves Anthony Burns and Thomas Simms. "Slavery," like the "Resistance" essay, spoke against the rule of "expediency" and "policy": "The law will never make men free; it is men who have got to make the law free" (Thoreau 2002, 193). The water lily, as previously noted, emerges near the end as a symbol of political rectitude—contrasting with the political muck, "the cowardice and want of principle of Northern men." The water lily resonates for Thoreau with the lotus of the Gita as a generic symbol for purity in men's thought and action (see chapter 6, "Purity"). The American flag was burnt in Worcester that day.

7. Between 1852 and 1854, Thoreau and his abolitionist confreres sided with and helped antislavery forces who were fighting with the pro-slavery "Border Ruffians." They bitterly opposed the Kansas-Nebraska Act of 1854, and welcomed John Brown, a leader of antislavery forces in Kansas, when he came to the Boston area in 1857 and 1859; he spoke to the Concord Town Hall on the former date and collected money on both occasions.

8. In 1859, John Brown and his twenty-one men were captured after seizing the munitions factory at Harper's Ferry in what was then Virginia. Thoreau went into overdrive during a uniquely agitated ten days of writing; his journal, for example, runs, "I put a piece of paper and a pencil under my pillow, and when I could not sleep I wrote in the dark," and, "There was a remarkable sunset, I think the

25th of October . . . but it was hard for me to see its beauty then, when my mind was filled with Captain Brown." On October 30 the selectmen once again would not permit the town bell to be rung, so Thoreau rang it himself before delivering "A Plea for Captain John Brown" to his fellow citizens.

After Brown's execution by hanging on December 2, 1859, Thoreau organized a funeral service in Concord, the town authorities notwithstanding. Again, he rang the bell.[2] "A Plea" was lectured days later in Worcester and in the Boston Temple of his abolitionist friend Theodore Parker. It was "reported, reprinted, and discussed in all the Boston papers" (Richardson 1986, 372). Like "The Last Days of John Brown," which appeared the next year, "A Plea" was published through many outlets and enjoyed enormous distribution in the Northeast. Its persuasive message was consistent with the Gita's: violence is bad, but social evil is worse.

The thesis of "A Plea" and "Last Days" was a Transcendentalist one. John Brown had "followed the voice within himself even though it led to opposition with the state" (Harding 1965, 418): "I see now that it was necessary that the bravest and humanest man in all the country should be hung" (Thoreau 2002, 279). The plea was also an appeal to Christian values, Thoreau likening Brown to Christ: "You who pretend to care for Christ crucified, consider what you are to do to him who offered himself to be the savior of four millions of men . . . Some eighteen hundred years ago Christ was crucified; this morning, perchance, Captain Brown was hung. These are the two ends of a chain which is not without its links. He is not Old Brown any longer; he is an Angel of Light" ("A Plea"; 2002, 147).

---

2. The fact that Thoreau three times took it upon himself to ring the bell in defiance of the selectmen, and got away with it, says much about his stature in the community.

These theses of "A Plea" were opposed by most fellow Concordians, even including, to some extent, fellow abolitionist Ralph Waldo Emerson, by the great majority of other abolitionists, including William Lloyd Garrison, and by antislavery liberals such as Abraham Lincoln—all of whom saw Brown as a threat to law and order in civil society. Of the "secret six" who had staked out Brown with arms and money, three fled the country (one helped on his way by Thoreau), two were jailed, and one was put away in an asylum for paranoia. Thoreau, in collusion with a "band of felons" and also subject to prosecution for treason, was according to one scholar "in danger of his life" (Reynolds 1998), not only from the government but from mob action. But he kept putting his spoken and written word into the fray and saw to its publication, assisted by Elizabeth Peabody, his sister Sophia, and other abolitionists. His lectures and his writings, his rhetoric, during and after 1859, did more than any other single factor to interpret and conceptualize the meaning of John Brown to fellow Americans so that, as the hymn goes, John Brown's truth went marching on, to Appomattox and the end of the Civil War in 1865—just as Thoreau's truth marches on to this day. The passive resistance of the "Resistance" essay and the advocacy of fighting a just war in "A Plea," though superficially divergent, even contradictory, were in accord with his deeper convictions as shaped by the Gita, where nonviolence (*ahiṃsā*) and "fight!" are recommended repeatedly in contiguous songs.

One must see the *Gita* effect in the larger context of striking common denominators shared by eight classics where, in each case, Thoreau selected and/or preferred one or two out of a range of options: Jeremiah, to begin, the fiercest and most categorical of the Old Testament prophets; St. Matthew (already emphasized in the present study), the most austere, severe, and moralistic of the Four Evangelists; among Classic Greek tragedies, Sophocles' *Antigone*, where the heroine, following her sense of right, insists on a proper burial for her brother—against a tyrant, and, as for Aeschylus, Prometheus, who defied the gods to give man, not just fire, but intelligence, the arts, and "blind hope"; among Shakespeare's plays it was "wild" *Hamlet,* the conscience-wracked individual versus a murderous usurper and tyrant; among many Chinese readings it was Confucius, especially the *Analects,* with their stress on duty in society; finally, it was the Laws of Manu, and, within the Gita, especially the first five songs and their concern with duty (*dharma*) and right action (*karma yoga*), that attracted Thoreau. All eight of Thoreau's preferences, then, have in common ethical action in terms of a demanding moral or legal code, in four cases facing off against a tyrant or a corrupt society. They also form a set with Luther and Plato (i.e., Socrates), both of whom are mentioned in *Walden.* The stern moral code at stake is consistent with some of the "absolutes" defined here in chapter 3—granted that this whole aspect of Thoreau has been obscured often enough by his stature as a consummate nature writer.

Gita, Gandhi, *Walden*, King: The Making of a Political Classic

The model carved out by Thoreau was matched, to begin, by the practice of Mahatma Gandhi in India. Gandhi must have known the Gita since early days, first studied it in earnest in London, then turned to it with renewed intensity during his first imprisonment in South Africa in 1908 (along with Tolstoy, Socrates, and others, of course). During the long years of struggle that culminated in Indian independence, he allegedly reread, memorized, and meditated on one stanza of the Gita per day.

> The Gita is the universal mother. She turns away nobody. Her door is wide open to anyone who

knocks. A true votary of Gita does not know
what disappointment is. He ever dwells in perennial joy and peace that passeth understanding.
But that peace and joy come not to skeptic or
to him who is proud of his intellect or learning.
It is reserved only for the humble in spirit who
brings to her worship a fullness of faith and an
undivided singleness of mind. There never was a
man who worshipped her in that spirit and went
disappointed. I find solace in the Bhagavad-Gita
that I miss even in the Sermon on the Mount.
When disappointment stares me in the face and
all alone I see not one ray of light, I go back
to the Bhagavad-Gita. I find a verse here and a
verse there, and I immediately begin to smile in
the midst of overwhelming tragedies—and my life
has been full of external tragedies—and if they
have left no visible or indelible scar on me, I owe
it all to the teaching of Bhagavad-Gita.[3] (Prabhu
and Rao 1968)

Gandhi's ideological grounding in the Gita early on
ran parallel with his study of Thoreau. "Why, of course, I
read Thoreau. I read *Walden* first in Johannesburg in South
Africa in 1906 and his ideas influenced me greatly. I adopted
some of them and recommended the study of Thoreau to
all my friends who were helping me in the cause of Indian
independence. Why, I actually took the name of my movement from Thoreau's essay, 'On the Duty of Civil Disobedience,' written about eighty years ago" (W. Miller 1938,
238–39). His reading of Thoreau was by no means limited
to these two works, however. As a result of correspondence
with the author he read H. S. Salt, Thoreau's excellent

---

3. Note that there are at least five allusions to the Gita as egalitarian,
even revolutionary (as was the Sermon on the Mount).

English biographer, "with great pleasure and equal profit" (Salt 1890, 100–101)—presumably including profit from its anarchical, anti-authoritarian gist. While in prison in 1908 he read Thoreau's essays, and quotes *Walden* extensively:

> He ended his account of his second jailing by adding, "Placed in a similar position for refusing his poll-tax, the American citizen, Thoreau, expressed similar thoughts in 1849. Seeing the walls of the cell in which he was confined, made of solid stone two or three feet thick and the door of wood and iron a foot thick, he said to himself thus: 'I saw that, if there was a wall of stone between me and my townsmen, there was a still more difficult one to climb or break through, before they could get to be as free as I was . . . I saw that the State was half-witted, that it was timid as a lone woman with her silver spoons, and that it did not know its friends from its foes, and I lost all my remaining respect for it, and pitied it.'" (Hendrick 1956, 471; and see Rossi 1992, 238)

Whether Thoreau initiated, catalyzed, or reinforced Gandhi's philosophy is secondary to the more basic point that, as Hendrick acutely concludes (1956, 471): "There can be no doubt that Gandhi was deeply indebted to the Thoreau who defied society and government to follow his conscience." Thoreau and the Gita contributed decisively to Gandhi's metamorphosis from respectable lawyer to radical political leader, and, indeed, a personification of "the Gita within *Walden*."

The foregoing on intertextuality and the interacting political action of both men can be nuanced by glances at how they enunciated the values in question. Gandhi was responding to a rhetoric that runs through Thoreau's writings. *Walden*'s first chapter, "Economy," criticizes and deconstructs the American political economy and its encapsulating materialism. It does this, in part, through a figurative and/or parodic exploitation of some two dozen key economic terms, such as "save" and "profit" (Cavell 1981, 88–89), which are interwoven with other sources such as the book of Matthew and economic theorists such as Adam Smith. The result is a synthesis of Juvenalian satire and Jeremian invective. Decisive examples of Thoreau's rhetoric also come from the just mentioned "A Plea for Captain John Brown," where, for example, he collocates three violent metaphors one after the other over ten lines: (1) "No doubt you can get more in your market for a quart of milk than for a quart of blood, but that is not the market that heroes carry their blood to"; (2) "when you plant, or bury, a hero in his field, a crop of heroes is sure to spring up"; and (3) the charge of seven hundred automaton brigadiers sung by a poet laureate is a less memorable feat than the charge of John Brown against "the legions of Slavery" ("A Plea," 2002, 267; alluding to "The Charge of the Light Brigade" by Tennyson). Thoreau, like Shakespeare, not only does not "block that metaphor," but mixes metaphors with wild abandon (Pesmen 1991). "A Plea" escalates further to a giddy sequencing capped with a metaphor that verges on catachresis: "I do not wish to kill nor to be killed, but I can foresee circumstances in which both these things would be by me unavoidable. We preserve the so-called peace of our community by deeds of petty violence every day. Look at the policeman's billy and handcuffs! Look at the jail! Look at the gallows! Look at the chaplain of the regiment! We are hoping only to live safely on the outskirts of *this* provisional army. *So* we defend ourselves and our hen-roosts, and maintain slavery" (2002, 276). Beneath Thoreau's *expressive poetics*, then, there roils the *persuasive rhetoric* that links *Walden* to Thoreau's political essays.

In the United States, Martin Luther King Jr. was inspired by both Thoreau and Mahatma Gandhi for ideas on civil resistance, nonviolence, and democratic liberation during the civil rights movement of the 1960s.[4] As mediated by these two men he was of course drawing on the Gita common to both of them. By 1994, the prime minister of India would state to a joint meeting of the United States House and Senate that "Henry David Thoreau was influenced by early Indian philosophy and thought," that "Thoreau influenced Mahatma Gandhi tremendously," and that "the United States and India have learned a great deal from each other throughout history" (Rao 2000).

Entering into this process of learning from each other, and the specific processes connecting political action and metaphysical speculation, Thoreau himself stated in an early (April 1840) journal entry: "The struggle in me is between a love of contemplation and a love of action—the life of a philosopher or a hero." This anguished struggle between action, to fight out of duty, versus the attainment of peace through meditation, also permeates the Gita. How the dilemma and the seeming disjunction were partly resolved by synthesizing a rhetoric of absolutes with the tropes and master symbols of a poetics has been one of the many burdens of the foregoing study.

---

4. It was my good fortune to hear him speak in Trivandrum, Kerala, India (where I was pursuing linguistic research): he alluded to *both* Gandhi and Thoreau.

Conclusions

Nobody except Van Doren and Sattelmeyer has ever seriously questioned that the Gita and, to a lesser extent, other Indian writings were highly significant to the conception and conceptualization of Thoreau's *Walden*. But scholars great and small have rarely stated how crucial it was or gone into the details or "the big picture," typically limiting themselves to naming the connection or pointing out a few formal features such as organization into eighteen units or a few themes such as the human—essentially Buddhist—despair with which both begin or the note of salvation or resurrection with which they end. The present endeavor has sought, in particular, by means of intertextual, philological, and symbolic analysis, to go far beyond these points and explore hitherto unnoted nodes and nooks and overarching and integrating constituents, thereby demonstrating a degree and depth of correspondence that has not been articulated previously.

I would first remind the reader that the Gita fed into *Walden* at all structural and epistemic levels, starting with the fairly superficial one of idiom, image, and trope as set forth in this study under, for example, "Eye and Light" and "Ax/Axis/Axes" in chapter 4. At deeper levels, the present book can be tallied up as follows, taking into account ethical absolutes, metaphysical concepts, and "the three ways to God," and integrating emotions.

Both books are governed by strong emotion often expressed by injunctions. Both books begin with a command to fight or, which amounts to the same thing, to strive and live on and survive despite any immediate vicissitudes or a generically bad milieu. In the same vein, both enjoin courage and honesty as unquestioned virtues and angrily condemn hypocrisy and all other false fronts and pretensions. Both advocate a wide variety of practices and exercises, physical or mental or both simultaneously, that, beneath culturally organized disparities, are actually analogous or, like solitary meditation, almost identical. For both books these ritualized practices have the ultimate goal of liberating the individual from delusion in general and, in particular, from the persuasive and habitual opposites such as joy and pain to which humankind is subject. In both books this freeing up from delusion and the practices that conduce to it leads to transcendental insight and knowledge, to truth that is revealed during ecstatic or at least emotion-charged events; concomitantly, both books disparage or bypass strict, logical reason and purely empirical experience as primary ways to truth and understanding. The attainment of revealed transcendental truth is, in the first instance, limited to a literary elite that can absorb the great books of the past. For both, the attainment of revealed truth enables the enlightened few to partly grasp the divinity of the individual self or soul and the divinity of the cosmos or oversoul: the individual spark and the great fire from which it emanated and into which it must eventually fall. In both books a second consequence of attaining revealed truth is the capacity, not only to see the universal spirit in the particular, but to see that all particulars are the same, to be indifferent to the differences between a Brahmin and a garbage collector, between a lotus and a loon. This realization of inner sameness implies an egalitarian overriding of literary elitism and is fully concurrent with the aforementioned denial of opposites.

Finally, liberation and the realization of truth are most likely and probable through the third way to God, toward which the argument or, better, the emotional trajectory and the persuasive magic of both books points. This third way is faith or loving devotion for a God in some sense. Faith or loving devotion outrank both disciplined practice and cognitive or logical knowledge. Both books explicitly or implicitly but always passionately urge on us this faith or loving devotion as a way of life and as a way to be reconciled with the absolute infinitudes, particularly the absolute infinitude of or at the moment of death.

Perhaps the deepest sharing by the Gita poet and Thoreau hovers between the dialectical and the downright contradictory: rebelliousness versus a certain conservatism, and this in turn points toward a yet deeper value that heads the reader/hearer toward a new view of life. The Gita, on the one hand, does advocate values such as those of the Vedas at many points and, more comprehensively, can be seen as a charter for doing one's duty within the framework of a caste system (Dasgupta 1965; Deepankar 2000), even if this means that as a warrior you will kill your kinsman: "Fight!" enjoins Lord Krishna. This same Krishna, however, is open to all humans irrespective of class or caste, gender or personal history, sinful or criminal or otherwise, whether Brahmin or outcaste cooker of dogflesh. By this reading it was a charter for Gandhi (1933). To make this revolutionary—for its time—point, the Gita poet jousts with and entertains conflicting and contradictory paths in a language that is itself replete with contraction, wild conjecture, and unsettling images. *Walden*'s Thoreau, and related writings, on the other hand, is rebellious and debunks hegemonic authority in its early environmentalism, its opposition to war, colonialism, and slavery, its juggling of diverse religions, its innumerable challenges to clichés and standardized practices, and far from least, its surreptitious and insidious poetics, its sometimes wild syntax and sometimes even wilder rhetoric, its exhortations to wake up, and its advocacy of an individualistic, self-reliant search for one's own, personal polestar. Yet at many points this same *Walden* extols unrestrained capitalistic trade, the westward expansion of the United States, and martial and entrepreneurial virtues of all kinds while appealing or alluding to conservative religious texts and an agrarian conservatism that harks back not so much to a generic Jeffersonianism as to Latin authors' nostalgia for the Golden Age of a patriarchal Republic. This dialectic in question is so extreme and pervasive as to make both books centripetal (conservative) and centrifugal (rebellious), driven by a double agenda: to hold the reader or audience, be it Hindu priests and warriors or Calvinist farmers and businessmen, by appealing to their deepest inherited values and symbols, while at the same time tearing off the veil of those values to reveal a radically new perspective or re-vision on how to live a better life in an ethical sense of practice and thought and a spiritual one of devotion to Krishna and Nature.

In the most general and abstract terms as well as many specifics of image and trope, then, the Gita is indeed "within" *Walden*; someone familiar with both texts can open the latter at random to any page and find or at least have intimations of the underlying, directive presence of the Gita within.

References

I have worked through the Sanskrit of the Gita three times over the past five years, memorized scores of stanzas, and read through and used all the translations listed here; van Buitenen and Edgerton strike me as the best all-around translations of the Gita, Miller as the most readable; Sargeant's multi-level version is priceless. Stanzas given without a credit line are my own translations, synthesized from the Sanskrit and at least three prior translations.

I have cited and used the canonical publications of Thoreau but for *Walden* have chosen the accessible and excellent Rossi (Norton) edition; most readers would prefer page citations rather than having to count paragraphs (if they haven't already done so) in the scriptural format of chapter and paragraph. In the same vein I have cited the recent editions of the generally fine secondary literature but have sometimes included older editions that I have used over the years, and the suggestive anthologies by Shepard and Stapleton.

Alcott, Louisa May. 1863. "Thoreau's Flute." *Atlantic Monthly* 12, no. 71 (Sept.).

Allen, Francis H. 1936. *Men of Concord by Henry D. Thoreau.* Illustrated by N. C. Wyeth. Boston: Houghton Mifflin.

Anderson, Charles R. 1968. *The Magic Circle of Walden.* New York: Holt, Rinehart and Winston.

Arapura, J. G. 1975. "The Upside Down Tree of the Bhagavadgita Ch. XV." *Numen* 22, fasc. 2: 130–44.

Barfield, Owen. 1971. *What Coleridge Thought.* Middletown, CT: Wesleyan University Press.

Bartscherer, Thomas. 2004. Personal communication.

Basham, A. L. 1956. *The Wonder That Was India*. London: Sidgwick and Jackson.

Benveniste, Emile. 1966. *Problèmes de linguistique générale*. Paris: Gallimard.

Bhattacharya, H. Principal. 1965. "Critical Observations on 'The Concept of God in the Bhagavad-Gita' by Patrick Olivelle." *Indian Philosophy and Culture* 10, no. 1: 29–46.

Blaisdell, Bob, ed. 2000. *Great Speeches by Native Americans*. Mineola, NY: Dover Publications.

Bonami, Andre. 2004. "Emerson, Thoreau, and John Brown—Kindred Spirits." Master's thesis, University of Chicago.

Boudreau, Gordon V. 1990. *The Roots of Walden and the Tree of Life*. Nashville: Vanderbilt University Press.

Brereton, Joel. 1990. "The Upanishads." In *Approaches to the Asian Classics*, ed. Wm. T. de Bary and I. Bloom, 135. New York: Columbia University Press.

Buell, Lawrence. 1973. "Catalogue Rhetoric." In *Literary Transcendentalism: Style and Vision in the American Renaissance*, 166–87. Ithaca: Cornell University Press.

———. 1989. "American Pastoral Ideology Reappraised." *American Literary History* 1, no. 1: 6–29.

Bush, Sargent. 1985. "The End and Means in *Walden*: Thoreau's Use of the Catechism." *Emerson Society Journal* 31: 1–10.

Cady, Lyman V. 1961. "Thoreau's Quotations from the Confucian Books in *Walden*." *American Literature* 33, no. 1: 20–32.

Cain, William E., ed. 2000. *A Historical Guide to Henry David Thoreau*. Oxford: Oxford University Press.

Cameron, Kenneth W. 1945. *Emerson the Essayist*. 2 vols. Raleigh, NC: Thistle Press.

Canby, Henry Seidel. 1937. "Prefatory Notes." In *The Works of Thoreau*. Boston: Houghton Mifflin.

———. 1939. *Thoreau*. Boston: Houghton Mifflin.

Carman, John B. 1987. "Bhakti." In *The Encyclopedia of Religion*, ed. Mircea Eliade, vol. 2, 130–34. New York: Macmillan.

Carpenter, Frederic Ives. 1968. *Emerson and Asia*. New York: Haskell House. (Orig. pub. 1930.)

Casagrande, Joseph B. 1960. *In the Company of Man: Twenty Portraits by Anthropologists*. New York: Harper.

Cavell, Stanley. 1981. *The Senses of Walden: An Expanded Edition*. Chicago: University of Chicago Press.

————. 2005. "Thoreau Thinks of Ponds, Heidegger of Rivers." In *Philosophy the Day After Tomorrow*, 213–35. Cambridge: Harvard University Press.

Christy, Arthur C. 1932. *The Orient in American Transcendentalism*. New York: Octagon.

Comey, Charles. 2004. "Creation, Destruction, and *Walden*'s 'Vital Heat'." Quarter paper, University of Chicago.

Cramer, Jeffrey, ed. 2003. *Walden: A Fully Annotated Edition*. New Haven: Yale University Press.

Dasgupta, Surendranath. 1965. *A History of Indian Philosophy*. Vol. 2. Cambridge: Cambridge University Press.

Davis, Melissa. 2002. "Meandering in Walden: Another False Bottom?" Quarter paper, University of Chicago.

Deepankar, Rahul. 2000. "Thoreau and *Gita* (Romanticism vs. Reality)." Quarter paper, University of Chicago.

Desai, Mahadev. 1951. *The Gospel of Selfless Action; or, The Gita according to Gandhi*. Ahmedabad: Navajivan Publishing House.

Dhawan, R. K. 1985. *Henry David Thoreau. A Study in Indian Influence*. New Delhi: Classical Publishing Company.

Diamond, Wai Chee. 2006. "Global Civil Society: Thoreau on Three Continents." In *Through Other Continents: American Literature Across Deep Time*, 7–23. Princeton: Princeton University Press.

Doniger, Wendy, and Brian K. Smith. 1991. *The Laws of Manu*. New York: Penguin Books.

Drinnon, Richard. 1962. "Thoreau's Politics of the Upright Man." *Massachusetts Review* 4, no.1: 126–38.

D'Sa, Francis X. 1985. *Word-Index to the Bhagavadgita*. Pune: Institute for the Study of Religion.

Duban, James. 1987. "Conscience and Consciousness: The Liberal Christian Context of Thoreau's Political Ethics. *New England Quarterly* 60, no. 2: 208–22.

Edgerton, Franklin. 1952. *The Bhagavad Gita*. 2 vols. Cambridge: Harvard University Press.

Eiseley, Loren. 1978. "Thoreau's Vision of the Natural World." In *The Star-Thrower*, 222–34. New York: Times Books.

Emerson, Ralph Waldo. 1966. "Thoreau." In Rossi 1992, 320–33.

————. 1983. *Essays and Lectures*, ed. Joel Porte. See esp. "The Poet," "Nature," and "Circles." New York: Library of America.

Fernandez, James W. 1986. *Persuasions and Performances: The Play of Tropes in Culture.* Bloomington: Indiana University Press.

Fischer, Elaine. 2003. "Thoreau's Middle Way." Quarter paper, University of Chicago.

Fliegelman, Jay. 1993. *Declaring Independence: Jefferson, Natural Language, and the Culture of Performance.* Stanford: Stanford University Press.

Friedrich, Carl J. 1950. *The New Image of the Common Man.* Boston: Beacon Press.

Friedrich, Paul. 1979. "The Symbol and Its Relative Non-Arbitrariness." In *Language, Context, and the Imagination: Essays by Paul Friedrich,* selected and introduced by Anwar S. Dil, 1–63. Stanford: Stanford University Press.

———. 1991. "Polytropy." In *Beyond Metaphor: The Theory of Tropes in Anthropology,* ed. James W. Fernandez, 17–56. Stanford: Stanford University Press.

———. 2000. "Ironic Irony." In *Irony in Action: Anthropology, Practice, and the Moral Imagination,* ed. James W. Fernandez and Mary Huber, 224–53. Chicago: University of Chicago Press.

———. 2004. "Tolstoy, Homer, and Genotypical Influence." *Comparative Literature* 56, no. 4: 283–99.

———. 2008. "*Walden's* Thoreau." Paper read at the Eighth Annual Gathering of the Thoreau Society. Concord, MA (July 11).

———. 2009. "Beyond the Unsaid: Transcending Language through Language." In *Theory, History, Exemplars,* ed. Ivo Strecker, Studies in Rhetoric Cutlure 1. New York: Berghahn Books, 2008.

Gandhi, Mahatma. 1933. *The Speeches and Writings of Mahatma Gandhi.* Madras.

Golemba, Henry. 1990. *Thoreau's Wild Rhetoric.* New York: New York University Press.

Gougeon, Len. 1990. *Virtue's Hero: Emerson, Antislavery, and Reform.* Athens: University of Georgia Press.

Gura, Philip F. 1981. *The Wisdom of Words: Language, Theology, and Literature in the New England Renaissance.* Middletown, CT: Wesleyan University Press.

Harding, Walter. 1965. *The Days of Henry Thoreau.* New York: Alfred A. Knopf.

Hegel, G. W. F. 1826. *On the Episode of the Mahābhārata Known by the Name Bhagavad-Gita by Wilhelm von Humboldt*, trans. Herbert Herring. New Delhi: Indian Council of Philosophical Research, 1995.

Hendrick, George. 1956. "The Influence of Thoreau's 'Civil Disobedience' on Gandhi's *Satyagraha.*" *New England Quarterly* 29: 462–71.

Hindus, Milton. 1971. *Walt Whitman, the Critical Heritage.* London: Routledge and K. Paul.

Hintze, Hannah. "Stevens's Still Lifes." MS.

Hodder, Alan D. 2001. *Thoreau's Ecstatic Witness.* New Haven: Yale University Press.

Hongbo, Tan. 1993. "Confucius at Walden Pond: Thoreau's Unpublished Confucius Translations." *Studies in the American Renaissance*, 275–303.

Huang, Chichung. 1997. *The Analects of Confucius.* New York: Oxford University Press.

Hume, Robert Ernest, trans. 1971. *The Thirteen Principal Upanishads.* London: Oxford University Press.

Izmirlieva, Valentina. 2008. *All the Names of the Lord: Lists, Mysticism and Magic.* Chicago: University of Chicago Press.

Jakobson, Roman. 1987. "Two Types of Language and Two Types of Linguistic Aphasia." In *Language in Literature*, ed. Krystyna Pomorska and Stephen Rudy, 95–121. Cambridge: Harvard University Press.

Jeswine, Miriam. 1971. "Henry David Thoreau: Apprentice to the Hindu Sages." PhD diss., University of Oregon.

Johnson, Barbara. 1987. "A Hound, a Bay Horse, and a Turtle Dove: Obscurity in *Walden.*" In *A World of Difference*, 49–56. Baltimore: Johns Hopkins University Press.

Johnson, Linck C. 1986. *Thoreau's Complex Weave: The Writing of "A Week on the Concord and Merrimac Rivers," with the Text of the First Draft.* Charlottesville: University Press of Virginia.

Johnson, William C., Jr. 1991. *What Thoreau Said: "Walden" and the Unsayable.* Moscow, ID: University of Idaho Press.

Kant, Immanuel. 1949 (1783). *Prolegomena to any Future Metaphysics that may be Presented as a Science.* Tr. and ed. Carl Friedrich.

In *The Philosophy of Kant: Immanuel Kant's Moral and Political Writings*. pp. 40–116. New York: Modern Library.

King, Martin Luther, Jr. 1986. *A Testament of Hope: The Essential Writings and Speeches of Martin Luther King, Jr.*, ed. James Melvin Washington. San Francisco: Harper.

Kluckhohn, Clyde. 1961. *Anthropology and the Classics*. Providence: Brown University Press.

Lamotte, Etienne. 1929. *Notes sur la Bhagavadgītā*. Paris: Librairie Orientaliste Paul Geuthner.

Larson, Gerald James. 2001 (1979). *Classical Sāṁkhya: An Interpretation of Its History and Meaning*. Delhi: Motilal Banarsidass.

Long, Larry R. 1979. "The Bible and the Composition of *Walden*." *Studies in the American Renaissance*, 309–54.

Macdonell, Arthur A. 1970. *A Vedic Reader for Students*. London: Oxford University Press.

McShane, Frank. 1964. "*Walden* and Yoga." *New England Quarterly* 37, no. 3: 322–43.

Mallory, J. P., and D. Q. Adams, eds. 1997. *Encyclopedia of Indo-European Culture*. London: Fitzroy Dearborn.

Marriott, McKim. 2003. "Varna and Jāti." In *The Hindu World*, ed. Gene R. Thursby and Sushil Mittal, 357–82. London: Routledge.

Matthiessen, F. O. 1941. *American Renaissance*. London: Oxford University Press.

Michaels, Walten Benn. 1977. "Walden's False Bottoms." *Glyph 1*, 132–49.

Milder, Robert. 1995. *Reimagining Thoreau*. New York: Cambridge University Press.

Miller, Barbara Stoller. 1986. *The Bhagavad-Gita: Krishna's Counsel in Time of War*. See esp. afterword, "Why Did Henry David Thoreau Take the Bhagavad-Gita to Walden Pond?" New York: Bantam Books.

Miller, Perry. 1967. *Nature's Nation*. Cambridge: Harvard University Press.

Miller, Webb. 1938. *I Found No Peace*. New York: Garden City.

Minor, Robert N. 1980. "The *Gita*'s Way as the Only Way." *Philosophy East and West* 30, no. 2: 339–54.

———. 1982. *Bhagavad-Gita: An Exegetical Commentary*. New Delhi: Heritage Publishers.

Moffitt, John. 1977. "The Bhagavad-Gita as Way-Shower to the Transcendental." *Theological Studies* 38, no. 2: 316–31.

Myerson, Joel, ed. 1988. *Critical Essays on Henry David Thoreau's "Walden."* Boston: G. K. Hall.

———. 1999. *The Cambridge Companion to Henry David Thoreau.* Cambridge: Cambridge University Press.

Myerson, Joel, and Philip F. Gura, comp. 1982. *Critical Essays on American Transcendentalism.* Boston: G. K. Hall.

Nietzsche, Friedrich. 1981. *A Nietzsche Reader.* Ed. R. J. Hollingdale. New York: Penguin.

Nodland, Ove Kenneth. 2003. "Deliberateness and Allegory in Thoreau's *Walden.*" Quarter paper, University of Chicago.

O'Flaherty, Wendy Doniger, ed. 1981. *The Rig Veda: An Anthology.* New York: Penguin Books.

Olivelle, Patrick. 1964. "The Concept of God in the Bhagavad Gita." *International Philosophical Quarterly* 4, no. 4: 514–41.

———. 1998. *Upanishads.* Oxford: Oxford University Press.

Paul, Sherman. 1953. "Resolution at Walden." In Rossi 1992, 349–59.

Pesmen, Dale. 1991. "Reasonable and Unreasonable Worlds: Some Expectations of Coherence in Culture Implied by the Prohibition of Mixed Metaphor." In *Beyond Metaphor: The Theory of Tropes in Anthropology,* ed. James W. Fernandez, 213–44. Stanford: Stanford University Press.

Plato. 1920. "Cratylus" and "Timaeus." In *The Dialogues of Plato,* trans. B. Jowett. New York: Random House.

Prabhu, R. K., and U. R. Rao, eds. 1968. *The Mind of Mahatma Gandhi.* Ahmedabad: Navajivan Publishing House.

Prabhupada, A. C. Bhaktivedanta Swami. 1972. *The Bhagavad-Gita as It Is.* Los Angeles: Bhaktivedanta Book Trust.

Preuninger, Joleen. 2004. "Thoreau's Faith in Walden and the Gospel of Matthew." Master's thesis, University of Chicago.

Pryor, Francis. 2000. *Seahenge: A Quest for Life and Death in Bronze Age Britain.* New York: HarperCollins.

Ramanujan. A. K. 1999. "Repetition in the *Mahābhārata.*" In *The Collected Essays of A. K. Ramanujan,* ed. Vinay Dharwadker, 161–84. Oxford: Oxford University Press.

Rao, P. V. Narasimha. 2000. "Speech to a Joint Meeting of the [American] House and Senate." MS.

Rayapati. J. P. Rao. 1973. *Early American Interest in Vedanta.* New York: Asia Publishing House.

Reynolds, David S. 1988. *Beneath the American Renaissance: The Subversive Imagination in the Age of Emerson and Melville.* New Haven: Yale University Press.

————. 1998. "How Radical Was He? Thoreau, the Transcendentalists, and Violent Abolitionism." Paper read at session 560, "The Political Thoreau." MLA Meetings, San Francisco, December 29.

Richardson, Robert D. 1986. *Henry David Thoreau: A Life of the Mind.* Berkeley: University of California Press.

————. 1995. *Emerson: The Mind on Fire.* Berkeley: University of California Press.

Riesman, David, in collaboration with Reuel Denney and Nathan Glazer. 1950. *The Lonely Crowd: A Study of the Changing American Character.* New Haven: Yale University Press.

Rossi, William. 1992. *"Walden" and "Resistance to Civil Government."* New York: W. W. Norton.

Roy, Rammohan. 1832. *Translation of Several Principal Books, Passages, and Texts of the Vedas, and of Some Controversial Works of Brahmanic Theology.* 2nd ed. London: Parbury, Allen & Co.

Salt, Henry S. 1890 [rev. 1908]. *The Life of Henry David Thoreau.* Reprint ed. by George Hendrick, Willene Hendrick, and Fritz Oehlschlaeger. Urbana: University of Illinois Press, 1993.

Sargeant, Winthrop, trans. 1994. *The Bhagavad Gita.* Ed. Christopher Chapple. Albany: State University of New York Press.

Sattelmeyer, Robert. 1988. *Thoreau's Reading: A Study in Intellectual History with Biographical Catalogue.* Princeton: Princeton University Press.

Schneider, Richard J. 1975. "Reflections in Walden Pond: Thoreau's Optics." *Emerson Society Quarterly: A Journal of the American Renaissance* 21, no. 1: 65–76.

Seybold, Ethel. 1951. *Thoreau: The Quest and the Classics.* New Haven: Yale University Press.

Shanley, J. Lyndon. 1957. *The Making of Walden.* Chicago: University of Chicago Press.

Sharma, Arvind. 1986. *The Hindu Gītā: Ancient and Classical Interpretations of the Bhagavadgītā.* La Salle, IL: Open Court.

Shepard, Odell, ed. 1961. *The Heart of Thoreau's Journals.* New York: Dover.

Shetty, Manu. 1995. "The *Bhagavad Gita* in the *Mahābhārata.*" In *Dialogism and Cultural Criticism,* ed. Clive Thomson and Hans Raj Dua, 149–75. London, Canada: Mestengo Press.

"The Shorter Catechism." n.d. In *The New England Primer.* (Twentieth Century Reprint). Boston: Ginn and Company.

Stapleton, Laurence, ed. 1960. *H. D. Thoreau: A Writer's Journal.* New York: Dover.

Stein, William Bysshe. 1963. "Thoreau's *Walden* and the *Bhagavad-Gita.*" *Topic* 6: 38–56.

———. 1967. *Two Brahman Sources of Emerson and Thoreau.* Gainesville, FL: Scholars' Facsimiles and Reprints.

Thoreau, Henry David. 1932. *The Transmigration of the Seven Brahmans.* Ed. Arthur Christy. New York: Wm. Edwin Rudge. (Trans. from M. A. Langlois's French trans. *Harivansa*).

———. 1980. *A Week on the Concord and Merrimac Rivers.* Ed. Carl F. Hovde, William L. Howarth, and Elizabeth Hall Witherell. Princeton: Princeton University Press.

———. 1981–2002. *Journal.* Vols. 1–8. Ed. John C. Broderick et al. Princeton: Princeton University Press.

———. 1988. *The Maine Woods.* New York: Penguin Books.

———. 1992. *"Walden" and "Resistance to Civil Government."* Ed. William Rossi. New York: W. W. Norton.

———. 1993. *"Faith in a Seed": "The Dispersion of Seeds," and Other Late Natural History Writings.* Ed. Bradley P. Dean. Washington, DC: Island Press.

———. 2002. *The Essays of Henry D. Thoreau.* Selected and edited by Lewis Hyde. New York: North Point Press.

Upadhyaya, K. N. 1969. "The Bhagavad-Gita on War and Peace." *Philosophy East and West* 19, no. 2: 159–69.

———. 1971. *Early Buddhism and the Bhagavadgītā.* Delhi: Motilal Banarsidass.

van Buitenen, J. A. B. 1998. *The Bhagavadgītā in the Mahābhārata: Text and Translation.* See esp. "Introduction," 1–31. Chicago: University of Chicago Press.

Van Doren, Mark. 1916. *Henry David Thoreau.* Boston: Houghton Mifflin.

158 References

West, Michael. 2000. *Transcendental Wordplay: America's Romantic Punsters and the Search for the Language of Nature.* Athens: Ohio University Press.

Whitehead, Alfred North. 1953. *Science and the Modern World.* New York: Free Press.

Whorf, Benjamin Lee. 1997. *Language, Thought, and Reality.* Ed. John B. Carroll. Cambridge: MIT Press.

Wilkins, Charles, trans. 1959. *The Bhagvat-geeta.* Introd. by George Hendrick. Gainesville, FL: Scholars' Facsimiles and Reprints. (Orig. pub. 1785.)

Williams, Paul O. 1963. "The Borrowed Ax—A Biblical Echo in *Walden?*" *Thoreau Society Bulletin* 83, no. 2 (Spring).

Wills, Garry. 2002. *"Negro President": Jefferson and the Slave Power.* Boston: Houghton Mifflin.

Wood, Barry. 1981. "Thoreau's Narrative Art in 'Civil Disobedience'." *Philological Quarterly* 60: 106–15.

Zaehner, R. C. 1973. *The Bhagavad-Gita.* London: Oxford University Press.

Zimmer, Heinrich. 1969. "Bhagavad Gita." In *Philosophies of India,* ed. Joseph Campbell, 379–400. Princeton: Princeton University Press, Bollingen Series.

Index

Page numbers with an *n* indicate footnotes.

9656543R0

Made in the USA
Lexington, KY
16 May 2011